MARK RAINSLEY

PADDLE SHAKESPEARE'S AVON

A GUIDE FOR CANOES, KAYAKS AND SUPS

First published 2022

Published in Great Britain 2022 by Pesda Press
Tan y Coed Canol
Ceunant
Caernarfon
Gwynedd
LL55 4RN

Copyright ©2022 Mark Rainsley

ISBN 9781906095857

The author asserts the moral right to be identified as the author of this work.

All rights reserved. No part of this publication may be reproduced,
stored in a retrieval system, or transmitted, in any form or by any
means, electronic, mechanical, photocopying, recording or otherwise,
without the prior written permission of the publisher.

Contains Ordnance Survey data © Crown copyright and database right 2022

Maps by Bute Cartographic

Printed and bound in Poland, www.hussarbooks.pl

📷 Great Comberton.

Foreword

There are few of us who live far from water. Our cities, towns and villages were built around waterways; our poorest, our most affluent and our most diverse communities are rarely far from water. Water provided the fuel that drove Britain's industrial history. Earlier in history, water provided our means of transport, trade, a source of food and importantly, a place for us to play and meet.

Our waterways have a magical way of drawing us in. We walk along their banks, we swim and paddle in their waters. From a canoe, one moves with the flow of water. Gazing outwards from a world where we are most used to looking in. You adventure to secret corners, where familiar surroundings can suddenly feel new and exciting.

The privilege of being a paddler or a swimmer can be both inspiring and frustrating in equal measures. There are rivers where paddlers and swimmers are forced to use stealth, or restrict themselves to the fringes of the day to avoid challenge or threat.

Why?

Because few of our rivers are fairly shared. They are guarded closely, to keep them off-limits to the public. Signs emit angry messages from the trees, prohibiting canoeing. From time to time an unfortunate paddler is confronted and informed that there is no place on the river for anyone with a paddle in their hand.

Living, paddling and raising two young sons alongside a river has given me a deep-rooted passion to find a way to address this inequity. Last summer, I watched my younger son run his fingers through the water as we paddled near our house. He sat up sharp as a kingfisher zipped past, a millisecond of blue reflected with instant wonder in his eyes. At four years old, my eldest son has paddled through clouds of mayflies in the evening sun. He has seen sand martins nesting and herons languidly launching into flight. One can never match these experiences in words and pictures, they only come from *being there*.

Like many of our rivers in Shakespeare's day, the Avon would have been a vital artery for trade and travel. It would also have been a place where people played and enjoyed being by the river. Thankfully, the majority of the Avon is still a draw for recreational activity, with rowing boats, cruisers, anglers, swimmers and of course paddlers, all sharing the space. In places like these, where people still have access to water, they feel a connection to it and are inclined to care about its health. Elsewhere, where that centuries-old bond between communities and their rivers has been broken, the public is growing increasingly disconnected from the fate of their precious blue spaces.

To my mind, the Clear Access, Clear Waters campaign has a simple aim; to ensure that the next generation – my sons and your children – can *be there*. In campaigning for 'open access' and the protection of our precious environment, we paddlers (and swimmers, walkers, whatever) have to be prepared to bear the responsibility of paddling with care, with consideration and with respect. Respect for nature, respect for others.

Changing government policy is a tall order, matched only by the challenge of winning the hearts and minds of those who wish to exclude us. Despite the scale of the challenge, we must take it on ... and we have done. Through our campaign – *your* campaign – we continue to lobby and press for a fair and equitable right of access to our inland waters.

Fair, shared, sustainable open access to water. It's not much to ask for. Is it?

Ben Seal

PLACES TO PADDLE MANAGER, BRITISH CANOEING

WWW.CLEARACCESSCLEARWATERS.ORG.UK

Ben Seal.

Contents

Foreword 4
Contents 6
Introduction 8
About the Author 9
Acknowledgements 10
Disclaimer 11

Avon Highlights 13

Shakespeare's Avon 17
An overview of the Avon 17
Climate and flows 20

Planning your Journey 23
Who? 23
When? 23
Which paddlecraft? 24
Carrying gear 25
Safety 25
Seeking help 31

Water levels 31
Rules of the river 32
Locks 33
Expeditions 35
Which bank? 39
Shakespeare's Avon Way 39
Maps 39

Access to the Avon 41
The Avon Navigation 41
The Upper Avon 42
Responsibilities 43
Further information 43

The Upper Avon 44
The Source 47
Section 1 – The Upper Reaches 53
Section 2 – Bubbenhall to Warwick 59
Section 3 – Warwick to
Stratford-upon-Avon 71

The Avon Navigation 82
Section 4 – Stratford-upon-Avon 85
Section 5 – Stratford-upon-Avon to
Bidford-on-Avon 95
Section 6 – Bidford-on-Avon to Evesham .. 105
Section 7 – Evesham to Pershore 115
Section 8 – Pershore to Eckington Bridge.. 127
Section 9 – Eckington Bridge to
the River Severn 137

Launching on the Avon 153
Launch points 154

Camping 159
Campsites 160

Culture and Landscape:
The Story of the Avon 163
Geology 163
History 164

Wildlife and Environment 175
Environmental issues 175
Habitats 177
Wildlife 180

Further Reading 184
Useful books 184
Historical sources 185
Essential reading 185

Index 187

Introduction

"I should say that for canoeists the Avon is one of the most beautiful rivers in England".

Luscombe, W.G. and Bird, L.J. *Canoeing*, 1948

Shakespeare's Avon is a great river to dip a paddle into, whether by kayak, canoe or paddleboard. Paddlers seeking an expedition journey, those wanting to just splash about getting wet and those participating in every kind of paddling endeavour in-between will find something for them on the Avon. From its upper rural reaches past Rugby and Coventry, through the villages and market towns of the south Midlands to its confluence with the River Severn on the floodplain at Tewkesbury, the river is, at all times, engaging to paddlers.

The Avon's natural wealth and beauty might come as a surprise to paddlers who imagine that the Midlands is all industrial cities! The riverine wildlife and scenery are always attractive, and at times truly stunning. In the half-century since the Avon was restored as a navigation, the deep channelled waters and the numerous locks, with their white-water interludes, have greened over into precious habitats for a range of flora and fauna.

A review of a previous river guidebook written by the author included the (perfectly reasonable) comment, *"Ah, too much history"*. Unfortunately for that paddler, the Avon has more history crammed along its modest length than it seems possible for any single river to bear. It flows right through England's past of climactic battles, monasteries, castles, stately homes and the early industry of mills and navigation … and we haven't even mentioned the Bard of Avon himself. The Avon's international fame is, of course, due to its associations with William Shakespeare, and whether or not you enjoyed your GCSE English lessons, it's impossible for paddlers not to get sucked into a little 'bardolatry' whilst enjoying the river.

This book aims to guide paddlers along the Avon and through its many locks and weirs, while also highlighting the river's remarkable natural and historical surrounds. I hope that it helps you to enjoy some great adventures on Shakespeare's river.

Mark Rainsley

About the Author

Mark Rainsley

Mark has spent over three decades using paddlesport as a means of avoiding adulthood and responsibility. He is a fanatical paddler who has descended challenging white-water rivers worldwide, and who is dedicated to exploring every nook and cranny of the UK's coast and rivers by kayak or canoe. He is a prolific contributor to paddlesport magazines and other media. Mark has authored numerous Pesda Press guidebooks including *South West Sea Kayaking*, *Paddle the Wye*, *Paddle the Severn* and *Paddle the Thames*.

The author.

Acknowledgements

It was Boxing Day, and my Christmas present had been a second-hand fibreglass kayak. My parents drove me outside Coventry to somewhere in the vicinity of Ryton-on-Dunsmore, launched me off at the first bridge they could find on the infant Avon and told me they'd meet me downstream somewhere. The river was flowing through barbed-wire fences along its sides and flooding across fields, I was wearing a woolly jumper and jeans and I'm not even sure that I had a buoyancy aid; welcome to 1980s parenting! By the time I met them at the next bridge, I was hypothermic, had blistered fingers and was hooked for life on paddling. Later, they drove me to slalom events at Stratford-upon-Avon and Luddington, and supported me in marathon races along the Avon. So ... thanks mum and dad, for helping me to start out in the sport and for getting me to the Avon.

Numerous friends and family came along and explored the Avon with me while I was working on this book; I'm lucky and grateful to have such great folk to paddle with.

"I count myself in nothing else so happy
As in a soul remembering my good friends."

Richard II

The following folk provided expert input; Ben Seal (British Canoeing's Places to Paddle Manager) was kind enough to write the foreword. Dr Lizzie Garnett offered input on geology. Heather Rainsley and Dick Whitehouse described their adventures on the Avon and Jenna Sanders offered advice on Duke of Edinburgh Award expeditions.

Finally, thanks to Franco Ferrero at Pesda Press, Vicky Barlow for her great design work, Don Williams of Bute Cartographic for the stunning maps, and Ros Morley and Andrew Whiting for their proofreading skills.

Photographs

All photographs by Mark Rainsley, except where acknowledged in the captions.

📷 *Evesham Weir.*

Important notice – disclaimer

Canoeing, kayaking and other paddlesports, whether in a river or sea environment, have their inherent risks, as do all adventurous activities. This guidebook highlights some considerations to take into account when planning your own river journey.

While we have included a range of factors to consider, you will need to plan your own journey and, within that, ensure there is scope to be adaptable to local conditions; for example, weather conditions and ever-changing river hazards (especially weirs!). This requires knowing your own abilities, then applying your own risk assessment to the conditions that you may encounter. The varying environmental conditions along the Avon mean that good judgement is required to decide whether to paddle or not.

The information within this book has been well researched. However, neither the author nor Pesda Press can be held responsible for any decision of whether to paddle or not, and any consequences arising from that decision.

Below Nafford Lock.

Avon Highlights

"The most peerless piece of earth, I think, that e' er the sun shone bright on."

A Winter's Tale

We hope that this book will inspire you to explore and enjoy as much of this wonderful river as possible. However, here are just a few suggested highlights to get you started ...

Meadows, woods and hills

Places of natural beauty to enjoy from the water or venture ashore and explore.

- Stoneleigh Deer Park (Section 2)
- Castle Park (Section 3)
- Cress Hill (Section 5)
- Marlcliff Corner (Section 6)
- Site of Cleeve Mill and Weir (Section 6)
- Bredon Hill (Section 8)
- Eckington Bridge (Sections 8 and 9)
- Severn Ham (Section 9)
- Harvington Lock and Weir (Section 6)
- Chadbury Lock and Weir (Section 7)
- Fladbury Lock and Cropthorne Mill (Section 7)
- Strensham Lock and weirs (Section 9)
- Abbey Mill (Section 9)

Locks, mills and weir pools

Attractive locks and weirs where you will want to linger. However, be extremely careful around the weir pools!

- Saxon Mill (Section 2)
- Lucy's Mill Weirs (Section 4)
- Welford Lock and Weir (Section 5)

Islands and secluded streams

Backwaters to escape boat traffic.

- All of section 1!
- Below Barford Weir (Section 3)
- Below Alveston Weir (Section 3)
- Binton Bridges (Section 5)
- Bidford Grange islands (Section 5)
- The River Arrow (Section 6)
- Osier and Tiddle Widdle Islands (Section 7)
- Below Nafford Weir (Section 8)
- The Mill Avon (Section 9)

Tewkesbury Abbey across The Bloody Meadow.

Picturesque cottages and churches

Villages where time has stood still.

    Ashow (Section 2)
    Welford-on-Avon (Section 5)
    Cleeve Prior (Section 6)
    Middle Littleton (Section 6)
    Offenham (Section 6)
    Cropthorne (Section 8)
    Great Comberton (Section 8)
    Eckington (Section 9)

History and culture

Engaging historical and cultural sites which can be appreciated from the water or via forays ashore.

    The Cromwell Memorial, Naseby (The Source)
    Stoneleigh Abbey (Section 2)
    Guy's Cliffe House (Section 2)
    Warwick Castle (Sections 2 and 3)
    Charlecote Park (Section 3)
    Bancroft Gardens and the Royal Shakespeare Theatre (Section 4)
    Abbey Park, Evesham (Section 6)
    Leicester Tower (Section 7)
    Pershore Abbey (Sections 7 and 8)
    Bredon Tithe Barn (Section 9)
    Tewkesbury Abbey (Section 9)

Clopton Bridge, Stratford-upon-Avon.

Shakespeare's Avon

"Avons winding streame,
By Warwick, entertaines the high complection'd Leame:
And as she thence along to Stratford on doth straine,
Receiueth little Heile the next into her traine:
Then taketh in the Stour, the Brooke, of all the rest
Which that most goodly Vale of Red-horse loueth best."

Poly-Olbion,
Michael Drayton, 1612

An overview of the Avon

Why 'Shakespeare's' Avon? Partly, to distinguish it from the eight other River Avons in Britain! Playwright William Shakespeare (1564–1616) grew up alongside the Avon, in Stratford-upon-Avon. Shakespeare was the greatest writer in the English (and perhaps any) language, but perhaps more significant is his legacy; he helped to define and shape national identity through his history plays and his development of the language. The Avon is hence inextricably linked to Shakespeare, and indeed the south Midlands region through which it flows is known as 'Shakespeare Country'.

Shakespeare's Avon is also known as the Warwickshire Avon or Stratford Avon. It is the longest of the Avons, measuring about 174km / 108 miles, and is the largest tributary of Britain's longest river, the Severn (which is also joined by the Bristol Avon). The Avon passes through four counties of the English Midlands (Northamptonshire, Leicestershire, Warwickshire and Worcestershire) to reach the fringes of South West England in Gloucestershire, descending from 190m at the source to less than 10m above sea level at the confluence with the River Severn. Its catchment is largely rural, but contains the conurbations of Coventry, Redditch, Rugby, Stratford and Warwick, with about 800,000 inhabitants between them.

📷 *Above Hampton Lucy on the Upper Avon.*

The Upper Avon

"*The Avon is canoeable from Rugby, but the stretch from that town to Ashow, near Kenilworth, should be undertaken only when the river is very full, otherwise there will not be enough water, and before the reeds have grown. ... It flows through lovely country ... Such great houses as Stoneleigh, Guy's Cliff, Warwick Castle and Charlecote lie close to the river and add interest to the cruise.*"

William Bliss,
The Heart of England by Waterway, 1933

Historically, Stratford-upon-Avon to Evesham on the Avon Navigation was known as the 'Upper Avon'. The Upper Avon is defined differently here, as the first 103km / 64 miles of the river *above* Stratford. This upper half is impassable to canal barges and other powered boats, but ideally suited to paddlecraft,

> ### "What's in a name?"
> *Romeo and Juliet*
>
> The word Avon derives from the Celtic *abona*, meaning 'river' (yes, it's the River River!). The Welsh *afon* and the Gaelic *abhainn* in Ireland and Scotland mean the same. On the continent, you'll encounter the Aven in Brittany, Avenza in Italy, Avona in Spain and so forth.

when the river has a moderate amount of flow from rainfall. From its source in the village of Naseby, alongside the Civil War battlefield, the Avon trickles through farmland to reach the town of Rugby. There is some adventurous (and surprisingly secluded) paddling to be enjoyed below Rugby, but as a 1924 Great Western Railway guidebook noted, "*It is not until it reaches Guy's Cliff, Warwick Castle*

Shakespeare and the Avon

Shakespeare did not mention or reference the Avon in any of his plays or sonnets ... or did he? Shakespeare scholars have pointed to the lines in *Hamlet* describing the death (possibly by suicide) of Ophelia ...

"There is a willow grows aslant a brook,
That shows his hoar leaves in the glassy stream.
There with fantastic garlands did she come
Of crowflowers, nettles, daisies, and long purples,
That liberal shepherds give a grosser name,
But our cold maids do dead men's fingers call them.
There on the pendant boughs her coronet weeds
Clamb'ring to hang, an envious sliver broke,
When down her weedy trophies and herself
Fell in the weeping brook."

Hamlet

They make the case that the 'glassy stream' which Ophelia falls into, with its willows and 'crowflowers' (water-crowfoot), sounds very much like the one that Shakespeare grew up alongside.

Intriguingly, in 1579 (when Shakespeare was fifteen) a girl drowned in the Avon just upstream of Stratford at Tiddington. Her body was exhumed for an inquest, which concluded that she, *"... by accident slipped and fell into the river ... and so was drowned, and not otherwise nor in other fashion came by her death"*. There are echoes of the gravediggers in *Hamlet*, who debate whether Ophelia is worthy of a Christian burial, given the rumours of her suicide.

The drowned girl's name, incidentally, was Katherine Hamlet.

Ophelia by John Everett Millais 1852 – Wikipedia Commons.

and Charlecote Park that the winding Avon makes good its claim to beauty and picturesqueness" (*Shakespeare-Land, The World's Great Travel Shrine*). These quiet reaches of the river between Coventry and Stratford, flowing through the almost-forgotten Forest of Arden, are exceptionally beautiful; adorned by landscaped parks, stately homes and ruins, and enlivened by exciting weir interludes, for those competent with white water.

Bubbenhall Bridge on the Upper Avon.

📷 *Binton Bridges on the Avon Navigation.*

The Avon Navigation

"There is little to say of the Avon below Stratford except that it keeps its particular and leafy charm every yard of the way ... it is all beautiful".

William Bliss,
The Heart of England by Waterway, 1933

The Navigation is the lower half of the Avon which has been made navigable to leisure craft by a total of seventeen locks and accompanying weirs. The Navigation officially starts at Alveston Weir, three kilometres upstream of Stratford; from Stratford to the River Severn at Tewkesbury is 71km / 44 miles. The Navigation follows a tortuous course trending southwest across England's rural heartlands, with stretches of secluded greenery interspersed by chocolate-box villages and small market towns; *"... if you land anywhere you like and walk up to the nearest village you will find England unspoiled"* (William Bliss, *The Heart of England by Waterway*, 1933). The frequently encountered locks, mostly unstaffed, are pleasant spots to find some shade and picnic, or maybe to cool down with a weir descent. Like its beginning, its end is at a battlefield; that of the 1471 Battle of Tewkesbury.

Climate and flows

"The rain it raineth every day"

King Lear

The Avon drains a catchment area of 2720 km², acquiring various small tributary rivers along the way (including the Leam, Stour, Sowe, Dene, Arrow, Isbourne and Swilgate). The average flow at Stoneleigh is about 2.5 cumecs (cubic

The Great Flood of 2007

On Friday 20th July 2007, 100.2mm of rain fell in Gloucestershire, three times the monthly average, in just seventeen hours. The rain fell onto saturated ground (27.6mm had fallen the day before) and flash flooding brought the Avon and Severn valleys to a standstill; cars were abandoned on the M5. Over the following 48 hours the waters rose further, high enough in Stratford-upon-Avon to flood the Swan Theatre and cancel their production of *Macbeth* (this was attributed to 'the curse of the Scottish play'). Downstream at the confluence of the Avon and Severn, Tewkesbury was totally submerged and the Abbey became an island; the Avon entered the church! The enormous Mythe Water Treatment Works at Tewkesbury were rendered inoperable on the 22nd, meaning that 150,000 homes had no fresh water supply for a fortnight. A worse disaster was averted when the Army and emergency services narrowly saved Walham sub-station in Gloucester; had the waters risen six centimetres higher, 350,000 homes would have been without electricity. 5,000 homes, 500 businesses and fifty schools were flooded in Gloucestershire alone. Three people lost their lives at Tewkesbury and another at Pershore, but the biggest peacetime rescue effort Britain has ever seen saved a great many vulnerable people.

metres per second), and by the time it reaches Warwick this has swelled to 8.2 cumecs. At Evesham, the average flow is 15.5 cumecs, with the highest discharge since records began in 1851 being 464 cumecs (!!!) during the 2007 floods. Close to the river's end at Bredon, the average flow is 16.7 cumecs; the Environment Agency don't attempt to measure high flows here, as in such times the Avon and Severn merge across the floodplain.

The Avon catchment area receives a moderate amount of rainfall, averaging from around 700–750mm annually. October and November tend to be the wettest months, but not notably so; the depressing fact is that it can rain year-round in the Midlands. Temperatures vary distinctly between summer and winter, due to the 'continental climate' effect of being far inland; they're not called the 'Midlands' for nothing.

Strensham Lock.

Pershore Bridges.

Planning your Journey

"It is one of those rivers which needs to be explored in a leisurely manner, both on account of its beauty of scenery and because of the richness of its associations in the story of England."

Alec R. Ellis, *The Book of Canoeing*, 1935

This section is intended to outline the factors involved in paddling on the Avon, whether you plan to splash about for simple fun, or whether you have grand expedition plans.

Who?

"The art of canoeing has no limits."

Arthur Quiller-Couch,
The Warwickshire Avon, 1892

The Avon is suitable for, and accessible to, all ages, genders and abilities. Complete beginners or novices on the Avon Navigation will find a perfect environment for learning and progressing quickly, provided they plan appropriately and take due care around locks and weirs. Paddlers on the Avon Navigation require a license; see page 41.

The Upper Avon is recommended to more experienced paddlers with understanding of how to tackle challenges and hazards such as trees, portages, moving water and, especially, weirs.

When?

The Avon Navigation is practical to paddle year-round, with the weirs holding back the water to maintain a depth of at least four feet. Excessive water levels are much more likely in winter; check the flow before paddling (see page 31). The Upper Avon will more reliably be practical to paddle during winter and spring, after recent rains have added decent (but ideally not excessive) flow. In summer, sections of the Upper Avon can become shallow or overgrown with reeds.

The angling 'close season' for the Avon is from 15th March until 15th June. Outside these four months, the Avon's banks will often be busy with anglers. Late spring (May to mid-June) is a particularly great time to enjoy the Avon; warm weather, healthy water flows, a quiet river and the river's natural environments at their green and glorious best.

Which paddlecraft?

"Light boats sail swift, though greater hulks draw deep."

Troilus and Cressida

Canoes are open-topped craft within which one or more paddlers sit or kneel, propelling themselves with single-bladed paddles. They are also known as 'open canoes' or 'Canadian canoes'. Kayaks can have closed decks or open decks (known as 'sit-on-tops' or SOTs) but the key difference is that the paddler sits, propelling him- or herself with a two-bladed paddle. Some kayaks have seats for more than one paddler. Just to complicate and confuse things, in Britain it is normal to use the word 'canoe' to refer to both canoes and kayaks!

Stand-up paddleboards (SUPs) are ubiquitous, now possibly outnumbering canoes and kayaks on the water. Their huge popularity (with a notable bias towards female participation) is partly explained by their accessibility (stand up, paddle) but also by the pure pleasure of traveling in this simple way, with an elevated viewpoint and your whole bodies' musculature actively involved, despite minimal connection to the craft. They are now commonly used for long trips and even multi-day expeditions. If shopping for a paddleboard, look for a model with a bit of length (10' 6" at least) for touring and decent deck elastics for carrying gear!

Which is best for the Avon? All are great. Canoes carry far more food and equipment, and are quicker to learn how to handle than kayaks. Kayaks are more manoeuvrable and less affected by wind, while paddleboards can be mastered quite quickly but are hard work in wind and limited in gear capacity. Paddleboards (with their fins) can't descend the weirs. Other kinds of paddlecraft are of course

The GWR Bridge below Stratford-upon-Avon.

available. Inflatable kayaks are, for example, common; a hybrid of raft and kayak. They are easy to transport off the water (onto trains and so forth) but slow and susceptible to the wind. The following books are recommended if you want to learn more about selecting and handling paddlecraft:

British Canoe Union Canoe and Kayak Handbook, Franco Ferrero (ed.), Pesda Press, 2002, ISBN 978 0953195657

Canoeing, Ray Goodwin, Pesda Press, 2016, ISBN 978 1906095543

Sit-on-top Kayak, Derek Hairon, Pesda Press, 2007, ISBN 978 1906095024

Carrying gear

Whether you are travelling for a day or a week, your equipment will need protecting and waterproofing. Canoes can carry watertight plastic barrels, which helpfully keep large amounts of gear dry and protected from knocks. A recent innovation is waterproof 60-litre duffle bags with a rolldown closure along the length of the bag; these are cheap and fit better in the canoe, but are not 100% dry if submerged. For kayaks and paddleboards, the best option is to use small and flexible 'drybags' which are sealed by a roll-top closure. These fit down the back of most kayaks and beneath paddleboard elastics, with a little persuasion. Unless you buy very expensive designs with watertight seals (e.g. those from Watershed Drybags), drybags are still likely to leak; consider putting your kit in thick plastic bags inside the drybags. Camera equipment and other fragile expensive equipment should ideally be protected in solid cases with padding, such as those produced by Peli Products. All of these barrels and bags will, of course, result in soaking or destroyed kit if you forget to close and seal them properly.

Safety

"Be wary, then. Best safety lies in fear."

Hamlet

This section is about *safety*: planning, selecting appropriate equipment, and understanding hazards encountered on the Avon to avoid getting into difficulty.

In normal summer water levels, the Avon Navigation is a forgiving and safe environment which is entirely suited to novices and the inexperienced, if a little common sense is applied in planning, selecting equipment and avoiding hazards. There are important caveats to this rule, however:

- A high water level exacerbates all normal hazards, making them harder to avoid and more consequential. We don't recommend recreational paddling on the Avon when it's at Red levels (see page 31) unless you are both very experienced and familiar with the river.
- The Upper Avon is a markedly different environment, being narrower and much less managed and maintained. Additional and sometimes unpredictable hazards include tree blockages, awkward portages, fast-flowing water and, especially, weirs.

Paddlers who want to learn more about the subject of safety (and rescue) are recommended to seek specialist training, or to consult *White Water Safety and Rescue* by Franco Ferrero (Pesda Press, 2006, ISBN 978 0954706159).

Clothing and equipment
Flotation
Canoes or kayaks must have some form of fixed buoyancy to prevent them from sinking when waterlogged. This is usually achieved through inflatable air bags, solid foam or sealed chambers in the boat.

Entrapment hazards
Make sure that any ropes, straps or suchlike are securely stowed away and cannot form a loop or point of entrapment / snagging for a paddler's foot or hand. Paddleboarders should consider using a waist attachment for their leashes, being easier to release in the event of snagging or entrapment.

Buoyancy aids
A well-fitted buoyancy aid is essential, and will make a swim much less dangerous. For the image-conscious, paddleboard buoyancy aids are available which can be worn unobtrusively around the waist and inflated by gas cylinders when needed.

Clothing
Your clothing needs to protect you from becoming hypothermic by remaining warm when wet and by providing a shield from the wind. Wetsuits do this well, but will probably be over-warm and restrictive in summer. An ideal solution could be to wear polypropylene or fleece thermals with a cagoule on top. Legs need similar protection, and don't forget a warm hat for your head! Helmets also retain heat well, and may be a good idea for young or inexperienced paddlers. Footwear should offer protection when scrambling ashore on muddy banks. You should also carry spare dry clothing.

Sun protection
Waterproof sun-cream and a brimmed hat will protect your skin and save you from the prospect of having to paddle with painful, chafing sunburn on the following day.

Phones
A mobile phone (packed in a waterproof case) is very useful to carry for summoning assistance in an emergency. Mapping apps can also help you to monitor your progress down the river.

River hazards
Weirs
"After all this peace comes now and again in delightful contrast those interludes in which the Avon so often rejoices; the white rush of the water over a long sloping weir of rugged stones, a fine spread of swirl and ripple over a gravelly bottom racing away in tortuous channels between small bosky islands of tangled verdure."

Arthur Granville Bradley,
The Rivers and Streams of England, 1909

📷 *Hampton Lucy Weir.*

The Avon Navigation's seventeen locks all have at least one man-made weir; an artificial dam holding back the water. There is an additional weir on the Mill Avon and at least sixteen more on the paddleable parts of the Upper Avon. The Navigation's weirs are all major constructions, while on the Upper they range from minor and almost unnoticeable, to fairly substantial. The Avon's weirs are not designed with paddler safety or enjoyment in mind, and all are potentially highly dangerous. Weirs can also incorporate all manner of user-unfriendly metalwork. Worst of all, the falling water loses energy by forming 'stoppers' – waves which fold back on themselves below drops, 'stopping' or even holding and drowning paddlers.

You will see many photographs in this book of the author's friends descending, or paddling near, the Avon's weirs. This is because they are all competent white-water paddlers with significant competence and experience acquired from descending white-water rivers internationally.

If you are not in a position of competence and experience to safely assess and paddle these potentially dangerous artificial structures, absolutely do not go near them.

If you want to learn how to assess and paddle white water safely, enrol yourself on a British Canoeing coaching scheme training course.

The weirs fall into a number of design categories:
- Sloping weirs – these have smooth faces and descend at relatively shallow angles; they can generate powerful stoppers at the base.
- Sloping weir faces with boulders lining the base – the boulders disrupt

the flow and form confused and unpredictable conditions at the base.
- Bouldery weirs – these are formed by walls of rocks simply laid across the river. The water flows between these rocks, sieve-like, and it is possible to trap or injure legs in the deep gaps between the rocks, if attempting to walk or wade on them. Bouldery weirs tend to generate several different channels of flow beneath them, as the water does not flow consistently along their face.
- Vertical weirs – these dissipate energy by plunging vertically over a sill, forming exceptionally powerful stoppers even in low flows.
- Sluices – almost every weir on the Avon has a channel leading to some form of sluice. This is a gate or tunnel, usually height-adjustable, to cope with varying river flows where water flows through to plunge over a vertical drop. Some sluices are hard to recognise, hidden behind barriers that the water flows strongly beneath. Sluices are exceptionally dangerous, certainly unpaddleable and are to be avoided in all circumstances.

Many weirs on the Navigation have floating barriers upstream of them, to deter leisure craft from wrong turns, and all have signage indicating where the lock channel is. These warnings give you plenty of space to avoid

Avon playspots

The Avon is unlike some rivers (notably the Thames), where the waves or stoppers below certain weirs form outstanding playspots for expert paddlers to surf. However, some play is possible at some weirs, with major care. The most popular playspot is Lucy's Mill Weir at Stratford Trinity Lock, where a friendly stopper and small surf wave appear at some levels. Nafford Weir (the sloping weir, *not* the main sluices) forms a powerful stopper which at certain levels is playable; at other levels, it most certainly is not. Some weirs (such as Luddington, where slaloms have been held) have several different focused channels at their base, making them good for practicing the basics of moving water. But that really is it; you will not find a Hurley or a Shepperton on the Avon. Plans have been mooted for a small artificial white-water course, to be built around Wyre Lock. As of 2022, the scheme was on hold.

Lucy's Mill Weir.

the weirs and find a safe channel. This can, of course, be a different story at high flows.

The Avon Navigation Trust prefer paddlers to portage the weirs. This seems a sensible policy, based on the reasonable assumption that most paddlers will not be in a position to judge the degree of risk. It is understood, however, that some of the weirs have for years regularly been descended by experienced local white-water paddlers, and have even been incorporated into regular canoe marathon races and suchlike.

The pools below weirs form some of the most beautiful spots on the river. Explore these in low water levels only, approaching from downstream, keeping a long way clear of the area affected by the weir current. The white water below certain weirs is carefully utilised for play by expert paddlers, in very specific conditions. Everyone else ... should steer well clear.

Obstacles

Be careful approaching the Avon's bridges, as the current piles onto the upstream side of the bridge pillars. These are usually designed to smoothly redirect water (and paddlers?), but some of the older bridges (such as Bidford and Eckington) are offset from the river's flow. They present a real challenge for leisure craft in higher flows; give them lots of room to line up and pass through!

Tree branches and other junk sometimes pile onto bridge pillars, causing a significant hazard. On the Navigation this is usually cleared quite quickly. On the Upper, trees can remain on bridges for a long period of time and even build up into substantial blockages. Tree branches and bushes lurk in the water along the riverbanks. Usually these 'strainers' are simple to avoid; however rivers flow towards the outsides of bends, and erode back the banks. In high water, you can find yourself being drawn towards or beneath overhanging foliage; steer to avoid. These hazards are a characteristic feature of the Upper, where low branches, overgrown bushes and even whole trees obstruct or completely block narrow points of the river – for example the channels below weirs. Totally avoid blockages, by portaging if necessary.

Moored boats, buoys and other fixed floating objects can be dangerous in high water. The current flows swiftly towards and under these things, with no cushion wave to push paddlers to safety – avoid!

Old Stare Bridge.

Wind

Wind is only a factor to consider in the final reaches of the Avon Navigation, where the banks open out (and a number of sailing clubs are based!). If you have a forecast of strong south-westerly winds (the prevailing direction), you may wish to adjust your plans. These conditions make paddlecraft difficult to steer, or even unmanageable.

Other river users

Powered leisure craft share the water with you on the Navigation. Most are competently and considerately handled, adhere to the speed limit and safely give paddlecraft a wide berth. Occasionally though, some do not fit this description; remain situationally aware and alert to what approaching craft might do.

"Every vessel shall proceed at slow speed not exceeding four miles per hour when passing moorings, small craft and vessels not under way ..."

Avon Navigation byelaws

On most stretches of the Navigation, moving traffic is usually light; you'll generally meet a boat or two at a lock, and then see nothing for a long while after. Those familiar with traffic on waterways such as the River Thames will find the Avon notably quieter.

Rowing boats are found training on a number of stretches, including the busy waters at Stratford-upon-Avon. Rowing eights travel at up to 15 knots / 28 kph, have their backs to you, and are pointy at the ends. Obviously, keep well clear of their path. If there is a risk of collision, shout out a warning or blow a whistle.

An additional issue to consider is anglers, between 15th June and 15th March. Avoid entanglement in lines by keeping a careful eye

Battling a headwind below Strensham.

Below Cleeve Hill.

out ahead. Pass wide around their lines and, obviously, pass quietly and considerately.

Seeking help

If you find yourself in serious difficulty and in need of assistance, do not hesitate to call the UK emergency phone number; 999. Give details of your group, your difficulty and perhaps most importantly, your location. The operator will summon the Police, Ambulance, Fire Service or Lowland Rescue as appropriate.

Water levels

'Rain added to a river that is rank
Perforce will force it overflow the bank'
                                        Venus and Adonis

To ascertain the level of the Avon before setting off to paddle, you have a number of options:

- Visit the Environment Agency (EA) Flood Warning Information Service website www.flood-warning-information.service.gov.uk/river-and-sea-levels and search for locations along the Avon.
- Call the Environment Agency Floodline on 0845 988 1188 to hear recorded information and advice (select option 1 and when prompted, dial 011131).
- Visit the Avon Navigation Trust's excellent Riverwatch website www.avonnavigationtrust.org/river-watch, which gives river level information and also links to live webcams monitoring the river.

The websites give readouts from numerous gauging stations along the Avon and its

Stratford Trinity Lock, note the coloured water level board.

tributaries. Looking at these graphs, you'll realise that the data needs to be handled with care. The system is set up to warn of floods, and major changes are needed in the river's flow before the graphs notably alter. The graphs show the height of the river level, not the volume of the river's flow. On the Avon Navigation, many sluices regulate the river level. This means that significant changes in the river's flow might not be reflected in the river level. The graphs for the Upper Avon are more reflective of change in the river's flow; avoid this section when there has been a recent sharp increase.

Each lock on the Navigation has a vertical coloured board at the exit gates, effectively a colour-coded river level gauge:

- Water within RED level: Danger present – river users should stop and moor their boats.
- Water within AMBER level: Increased current – proceed with caution.
- Water within GREEN level: Normal navigation level.

Rules of the river

The Avon Navigation Trust has a number of simple rules for all watercraft to obey:
- Keep to the right of the channel and pass other craft to port (drive on the right).
- Powered craft should indicate their intentions by short whistle blasts:
  - One blast – I am changing course to starboard (right).
  - Two blasts – I am changing course to port (left).
  - One long blast, two short blasts – I'm a wide vessel, I need the whole river.

- Keep to the speed limits:
    - 4 mph heading upstream.
    - 6 mph heading downstream.
    - 3 mph at Stratford-upon-Avon.
    - 4 mph when passing moorings, anglers and small craft (paddlecraft!).
- All vessels should carry a lifejacket or similar for every passenger (or a lifebuoy for every two).
- After dark, all powered craft should show lights. Paddlecraft should show a single white light when in the vicinity of another moving vessel.

The Avon Navigation Trust have a phoneline for reporting concerns or incidents; 0300 999 2010. In addition, there is an Environment Agency Hotline to report damage or danger to the environment, damage to structures or water escaping; 0800 80 70 60.

Locks

The locks are an attractive feature of the Avon Navigation's landscape and can even be a social hub where you get a chance to catch up with other water users. The lock names are highlighted in bold in each river section to help you locate them easily. See the table overleaf for page numbers.

There are seventeen locks in total, with the additional (immense) Upper Lode Lock to negotiate on the River Severn if you finish your Avon journey (see Section 9) on that river. The majority are manually operated, with only Evesham and Avon (Tewkesbury) staffed by lock keepers. All of the Avon's locks can be portaged; some have landing stages to leave the water on the lock's upstream side, and jetties downstream to launch from. It must be noted that some of these locks are more user-friendly to portage than others, so be prepared for a bit of lifting and hauling; ropes on bows and sterns are helpful. Obviously, portaging around locks can be awkward with a heavy paddlecraft; a trolley is recommended for canoes. A few locks have portage trails close to water level, following the weir face.

The Avon Navigation Trust ask paddlers (and all unpowered craft) not to enter the locks. The experience of the author and his friends is that this is sound advice. A surprising lesson learned from using paddlecraft in the Avon locks (and from watching leisure craft passing through alone) is that you cannot assume that any leisure craft with which you might share the lock chambers is crewed competently and safely. We have witnessed some alarming incompetence or negligence, which would potentially subject paddlers to dangerous 'Star Wars Garbage Compactor' experiences. If you must use the locks, enter the chambers alone and operate them independently, at a time when there is no other traffic around whom you might delay.

The procedure for operating the locks (going downstream) is as follows:

Fill the chamber if needed. Open both top gates. Enter and secure yourself. Close the top gates. Operate the rack gearing to close the top gate. Check no boats are downstream of the bottom gate. Open the paddles on the lower gate (a little at first, then when the water settles, all the way). Open the bottom gates, leave. Close all paddles, leave the bottom gate open.

Lock keys of the standard 1-inch taper BCN type are needed to operate the locks. These can be purchased from the Stratford Waterways Information Centre (see Section 4) or from the lock keeper at Avon Lock in Tewkesbury.

Children should be supervised at all times when visiting lock sites, and running on the lock side is not permitted.

No	Lock	Grid reference	Drop	Distance from previous lock	Distance from the source of the Avon	Water point	Other details	Page number
1	Stratford Trinity	SP 201 542	4' 11"	0km	103.5km			90
2	Weir Brake	SP 199 536	2' 11"	0.8km	104.3km			96
3	Luddington	SP 166 523	6' 3"	3.6km	107.9km	Y		98
4	Welford	SP 143 520	7' 1"	4.9km	112.8km			99
5	Bidford Grange	SP 120 517	2' 7"	2.6km	115.4km			101
6	Barton	SP 107 513	2' 8"	1.5km	116.9km			101
7	Marlcliff	SP 088 506	5'	2.9km	119.8km			107
8	Harvington	SP 065 477	3' 4"	4.5km	124.3km			108
9	Offenham	SP 064 471	3' 2"	0.7km	125km	Y		109
10	Evesham	SP 041 438	7'3"	5.5km	130.5km	Y	Lock keeper: 01386 446511	112
11	Chadbury	SP 025 460	5'	5km	135.5km			118
12	Fladbury	SO 997 461	7' 6"	4.4km	139.9km			121
13	Wyre	SO 959 469	3' 6"	7km	146.9km			123
14	Pershore	SO 952 456	9'	1.7km	148.6km			128
15	Nafford	SO 940 418	5' 6"	8.2km	156.8km			132
16	Strensham	SO 915 404	4'	5.7km	162.5km	Y		140
17	Avon	SO 892 331	7' 6"	9km	171.5km	Y	Lock keeper: 01684 292129	145

Expeditions

"To unpath'd waters, undream'd shores..."
The Winter's Tale

A multi-day paddle on the Avon is highly recommended and will reward you with some lovely experiences to fill out your memory bank! There are lots of possibilities for overnight mini-adventures. Paddling the whole length of the Avon Navigation is a splendid challenge. Motivated paddlers on a monomaniacal mission could possibly conquer the entire Navigation in a weekend, but they would miss so much; take a bit longer to explore and absorb.

This book's guides to sections of the Avon are of course paddling trip itineraries, each lasting from half a day to a day. Suggested here is a possible itinerary which joins these into a multi-day expedition along the Avon Navigation, based around the locations of riverside campsites (book well ahead!). The daily distances are inconsistent, but reflect the available campsites. The itinerary gives plenty of time to portage or paddle weirs and explore ashore. Consider adding an extra day at the start to 'do culture' in Stratford-upon-Avon and definitely factor in an ascent of Bredon Hill along your way.

There is the possibility of continuing further downstream to Gloucester or Maisemore on the River Severn, taking care at the major weirs where the river becomes tidal. Paddling even further to the sea at Sharpness is feasible; see *Paddle the Severn* by Mark Rainsley.

The notable limitation to planning multi-day expeditions which also include the Upper Avon is the limited range of public campsites along these stretches, coupled with the fact that the higher water levels needed for much of it are generally found in the winter months. Nevertheless, a well-organised and motivated group could add the wonderful paddle from Warwick (or Barton?) to Stratford, which is possible year-round, to the above itinerary; the key challenge is managing the very early start (see Section 3).

Day	From	To	Campsite	Distance	Distance from source
1	Stratford-upon-Avon	Barton Lock	Cottage of Content	13.4km	116.9km
2	Barton Lock	Evesham Lock	Evesham Caravan Site	13.6km	130.5km
3	Evesham Lock	Wyre Lock	Wyre Mill Club	16.4km	146.9km
4	Wyre Piddle Lock	Strensham Lock	Andrew's Field	15.6km	162.5km
5	Strensham Lock	Lower Lode	Lower Lode Inn	11.5km	174km

Paddleboarding the Avon

I wasn't sure it seemed like a good idea. Paddleboard every day for a week? Was it something I could do? I had only paddleboarded brief stretches of river and coast before, perhaps for an hour or so. Although there are amazing paddleboarders who have paddled Land's End to John O'Groats and the like, in my mind paddleboarding was still a way to cool off at the beach on a hot Saturday afternoon.

What grabbed my interest was the prospect of a journey. A journey down a river I knew nothing about. I'm not someone who can exercise for the sake of exercise, there has to be something more to it. Boris's Covid lockdown 'daily exercise' was disastrous for me as a way of keeping fit; no purpose, no point, no goal. What motivates me is making a journey and discovering things along the way. So, I realised that I had talked myself into it.

Fast-forward a few months and a tiny bit of distance training (see above, to explain the 'tiny' bit). I found myself in Stratford-upon-Avon with my paddleboard, my paddle and a collection of friends. After the long winter lockdown I felt dazed, both by the hot sunny weather and the crowds of tourists. Our motley crew of kayaks, canoes and paddleboards launched and manoeuvred amongst rowing sculls and menacing swans.

Journeying down the Avon from Stratford to the confluence with the Severn (and then down the Severn to sea level at Maisemore) was a wonderful six days of paddling. Each day was an immersion in a watery corridor, separate from the land-based world through which we floated. Towns, villages, farmland, woodland, abbeys, mills, weirs, waterfront pubs and everything in-between

Duke of Edinburgh's Award expeditions

"Screw your courage to the sticking place,
And we'll not fail."

Macbeth

The Duke of Edinburgh's Awards for 14–24 year olds are intended to, *"inspire, guide and support young people in their self-development"*. A key component of the awards is, *"To inspire young people to develop initiative and a spirit of adventure and discovery, by planning, training for and completing an adventurous self-sufficient journey, as part of a team"*.

The Avon Navigation sees use by DofE expedition groups for expedition training or for final qualifying expeditions. The river suits this for a range of reasons; it flows through areas fitting the DofE's definitions of 'rural', there is an undisputed right of navigation, riverside campsites are available at intervals, equipment and guides / instructors are available to hire and it is easy for a DofE Supervisor to monitor a group's progress from bridges, locks and footpaths such as the Shakespeare's Avon Way.

paraded past. At times, the wind was in our faces and we slowed down ... but when it was behind us, we paddleboarders suddenly found ourselves much faster than everyone else due to our body-shaped sails.

There is a bit of a process to portaging a paddleboard around weirs and locks. The first few times, I made more of a meal of it than necessary. There's the bit where you try to approach the mooring wall at the right speed and angle, so you don't crash and fall over. Then there's the bit where you temporarily attach your board to the bank, whilst you faff with your stuff; this is where advice from a friend to carry carabiners and a climbing sling came in very handy. Then you lift your stuff (picnic, sun cream, water bottle and kitchen sink) onto the bank and gracefully (not always in my case) climb up to join it. Then you use the sling to pull your board up. Then you help everyone else. Then, you carry everything around the lock ... and repeat the whole process in reverse. Every time I think of that week, so many memories stand out: picnics in the shade on beautifully mowed lawns at locks; swims in the river to cool off; admiring and coveting the various watercraft that ploughed their way along the Navigation with us; deer quietly browsing in a woodland; banks of shells below many of the weirs, hinting that you may be lucky enough to spot an otter eating there, if you were early or late enough; and the honks of geese as they settled down for the night near our camps.

The Avon is no longer an unknown, but there is so much I want to go back and see again.

Heather Rainsley

The award criteria overleaf are met by different sections of the Avon Navigation, with the Silver Award expedition requirements closely adhering to the length of the Navigation. For a Gold Award expedition, further mileage would be required, perhaps achieved by continuing past downstream on the River Severn; this could involve some potentially challenging tidal conditions after Gloucester.

The Avon has excellent potential for selecting engaging and challenging expedition aims. The wildlife and environment are easy to access and observe, while the region's history and culture offer more ideas; why not investigate the fate of the three Abbeys, or the wildlife around the restored locks, for example?

Further advice on DofE expeditions over water can also be found in Chapter 13 of the *Expedition Guide*:

The Duke of Edinburgh's Award Expedition Guide, Alex Davies, The Award Scheme Ltd., 2019, ISBN 978 0 905425 20 7

Award	Recommended environment	Duration of expedition	Advised distances
Bronze	Canals, rivers or other inland waterways and lakes. The water and area may be familiar to participants.	2 days, 1 night, 6 hours of planned activity daily	16–20km daily, 32–40km total
Silver	Canals, rivers or other inland waterways and lakes in rural areas. The water must be unfamiliar to the participants and present an appropriate challenge. There is an expectation that the conditions will be related to the age and experience of the participants and represent a progression between Bronze and Gold.	3 days, 2 nights, 7 hours of planned activity daily	22km daily, 65km total
Gold	Rivers or other inland waterways and lakes in rural areas, sheltered coastal waters or estuaries. The water must be unfamiliar to the participants and must present an appropriate challenge. At Gold level routes should be in, or pass, through wild country. Moving water, either by current or tide, or large bodies of water, should be sought where possible.	4 days, 3 nights, 8 hours of planned activity daily	32km daily, 128km total

"I really love the Avon for DofE Bronze and Silver expeditions. It gently winds its way through beautiful countryside, and often feels far more remote than it actually is. The many locks and weirs offer some interesting diversions, as does the river life, with plenty of wildlife to be enjoyed and passing narrowboats to share smiles with.

During Covid, it offered a lifeline to our Gold groups, allowing them to get their (already postponed) practice expeditions done locally enough to allow for them to sleep at home; a very strange DofE experience, but one that was so important, not only as a means to the end goal of enabling a qualifying expedition, but also for the tangible difference it made to a group of teenagers to be able to get out of the house and fully outdoors for a few days."

Jenna Sanders, DofE expedition provider
Flying Gecko Outdoors,
www.flyinggeckooutdoors.co.uk

Which bank?

Throughout this book, the terms 'river left' and 'river right' are commonly used to locate features. 'River left' is simply the left-hand bank when you are looking downstream, and 'river right' is ... okay, you get it.

Shakespeare's Avon Way

Shakespeare's Avon Way is a 142km waymarked long-distance trail from the Avon's source at Naseby to its end at Tewkesbury. Some stretches adhere closely to the course of the river, whilst others veer for a considerable distance 'inland', determined by the available Public Rights of Way. Various stretches of the trail would work well to provide a 'walking shuttle', for example along Sections 5 and 6. The route is shown on Ordnance Survey maps and is waymarked clearly on the ground.

More information is available from the Shakespeare's Avon Way Association's website www.shakespearesavonway.org and from their guidebook:

Shakespeare's Avon Way, a Walk through History, Jenney Davidson, The Macmillan Way Association, 2008, ISBN 0952685167

Maps

The maps in this book are more than adequate to find your way along the River Avon. Ordnance Survey maps offer additional detail; the table below lists which OS maps cover each section of the river. Waterway Routes sell high quality maps of the Navigation showing locks and other features, which can be used on phones and other devices. The maps are downloadable from their website www.waterwayroutes.co.uk.

Section	1:50000 Landranger map(s)	1:25000 Explorer map(s)
Source	141, 140	223, 222
1	140	222, 221
2	140, 151	221
3	151	221, 205
4	151	205
5	151, 150	205
6	150	205
7	150	205, 190
8	150	190
9	150	190

Bubbenhall on the Upper Avon.

Access to the Avon

"The said river Avon shall forever thereafter be accounted and be a free river and all and every person and persons shall have liberty of passing and re-passing up and down the said river with boats, barges, lighters and other vessels."

Act of Parliament 1751

The Avon Navigation

From Alveston Weir downstream to the River Severn, the Avon is subject to an undisputed Public Right of Navigation (PRN). This means that there are no restrictions on paddling the Avon Navigation other than the need to acquire a license:

- Licenses can be obtained from the Avon Navigation Trust either online or at the Stratford Waterways Information Centre (their canal barge in Bancroft Basin) and Avon Lock at Tewkesbury. Day licenses cost just a few pounds; the only awkward bit is that you have to prove that you have third party insurance.
- Paddlers who join British Canoeing (formerly known as the British Canoe Union) don't need to buy a license. British Canoeing membership includes a license for the Avon, along with third party insurance. Simple.

Only Evesham and Avon Locks are staffed; at these locations you may be asked to show your license or British Canoeing membership card. Paddlers completing the Avon by paddling through enormous Lower Lode Lock on the River Severn (see Section 9) will need either British Canoeing membership or a license from the Canal & River Trust and will likely be asked to show this. Paddling on the Stratford-upon-Avon Canal also requires either British Canoeing membership or a Canal & River Trust license.

What this means, simply, is that you can paddle freely year-round, and that **your basic right to enjoy your river heritage is legally enshrined**.

Charlecote Park.

Note that this does not give you right of access to the riverbank. Also, mill ponds and backwaters around locks and weirs are not included within the Navigation, so your right to paddle here is not yet legally enshrined.

The Upper Avon

The right to enjoy your river heritage on the Avon upstream of Alveston is disputed by some. However, this certainly does not mean that doing so is illegal.

> *"British Canoeing believes that there is a strong case to demonstrate an existing public right of navigation (PRN) on all navigable rivers."*
>
> British Canoeing

There are a number of signs (some farcically large) on the Upper Avon which state that enjoying your river heritage by paddlecraft is not allowed, or that permission should be sought from such and such. It is extremely important to understand that these signs have zero legal validity. They represent an opinion, a worldview and an aspiration, not the law.

> *"British Canoeing believes, based on a wealth of historical evidence, that there is, under common law, a public right of navigation on all rivers which are physically capable of being navigated. It is acknowledged that this position is firmly rejected by others."*
>
> British Canoeing,
> *Access and Environment Charter*

Disregard the signs and use your own discretion and common sense in deciding how best to enjoy your river heritage. Note also the specific advice relating to access in the respective river sections in this book.

"Boldness be my friend!
Arm me, audacity, from head to foot!"

Cymbeline

> In the unlikely event that you are challenged whilst paddling the Avon, be polite and respectful, but do not be dissuaded from enjoying your river heritage. Should you find your path physically barred by individuals, or if you feel threatened, report this to the police just as you would in any other part of life. Also, log any incidents with British Canoeing, who have a form for such purposes on their website.

Responsibilities

It should go without saying that your basic right to enjoy your river heritage comes with responsibilities; most importantly, to respect and preserve the river environment for its own sake, and for others to enjoy. The passage of paddlecraft *by definition* has minimal impact upon the riverine environment, but employ common sense to ensure that this always and absolutely remains the case. Be prepared to pick up and remove other people's waste when you encounter it; angling and agricultural detritus is sadly not uncommon.

Some sensible advice can be found in the British Canoeing leaflet *You, your canoe and the environment*, downloadable from their website.

Further information

www.britishcanoeing.org.uk – British Canoeing
www.avonnavigationtrust.org – The Avon Navigation Trust
www.canalrivertrust.org.uk – The Canal & River Trust (River Severn and Stratford-upon-Avon Canal)
www.riveraccessforall.co.uk – Access to British Rivers

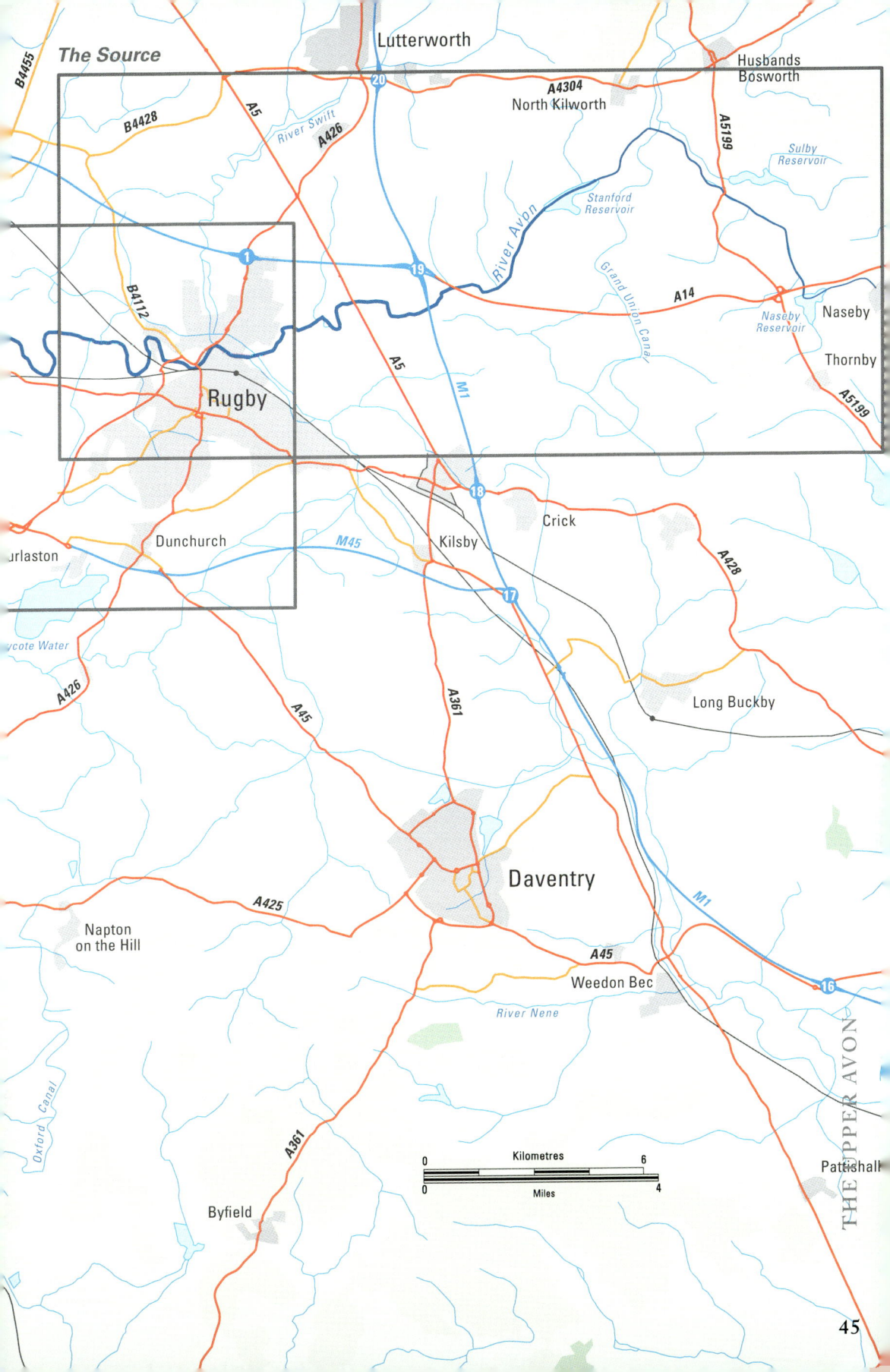

Cromwell Memorial, Naseby.

Lilbourne.

The Source

The Source

Distance 33.5km
Start △ The Source, Naseby SP 688 782 / NN6 6DF
Finish ○ Newbold on Avon SP 490 770 / CV21 1EF

Introduction

The Avon rises in the village of Naseby in Northamptonshire. For its first 30 kilometres to the town of Rugby it is a barely noticeable stream and probably not worth paddling. However, a morning spent investigating the Avon's origins by cycle or car makes for an engaging prelude to descending the river below Rugby (Section 1).

Waypoints above Rugby

The Source, Naseby SP 688 782 / NN6 6DF
Welford SP 645 807 / NN6 6JQ
Stanford Reservoir SP 611 811 / LE17 6DY
Stanford Hall SP 587 788 / NN6 6JP
Lilbourne SP 559 775 / CV23 0SX

Description

Outlined here are a few waypoints along the infant Avon, all visitable by road. It is possible to explore the area further by footpath and bridleway; however hardly any more of the river will be seen.

The Avon rises in the village of Naseby, at 193m above sea level. This is almost the highest point in Northamptonshire and the source of the River Nene is only a kilometre to the east (the Nene reaches The Wash after 160km). Naseby is of course famous as the location of the Civil War battle. The Avon's source spring is marked by a strange cast iron cone marked *'Source of the Avon 1822'*, located in a private

47

garden, across Welford Road from All Saints Church. Water once bubbled from the cone, but (after a nearby housing development) has not done so for decades.

The Avon trickles into Naseby Reservoir and then re-emerges to reach the village of Welford (not to be confused with Welford-on-Avon, see Section 5), 6.7km from the source. This is the terminus of the Grand Union Canal's Welford Branch. The canal basin is a pleasant hub, overlooked by the Wharf Inn which sits on the Northamptonshire / Leicestershire border; the

The source spring, Naseby.

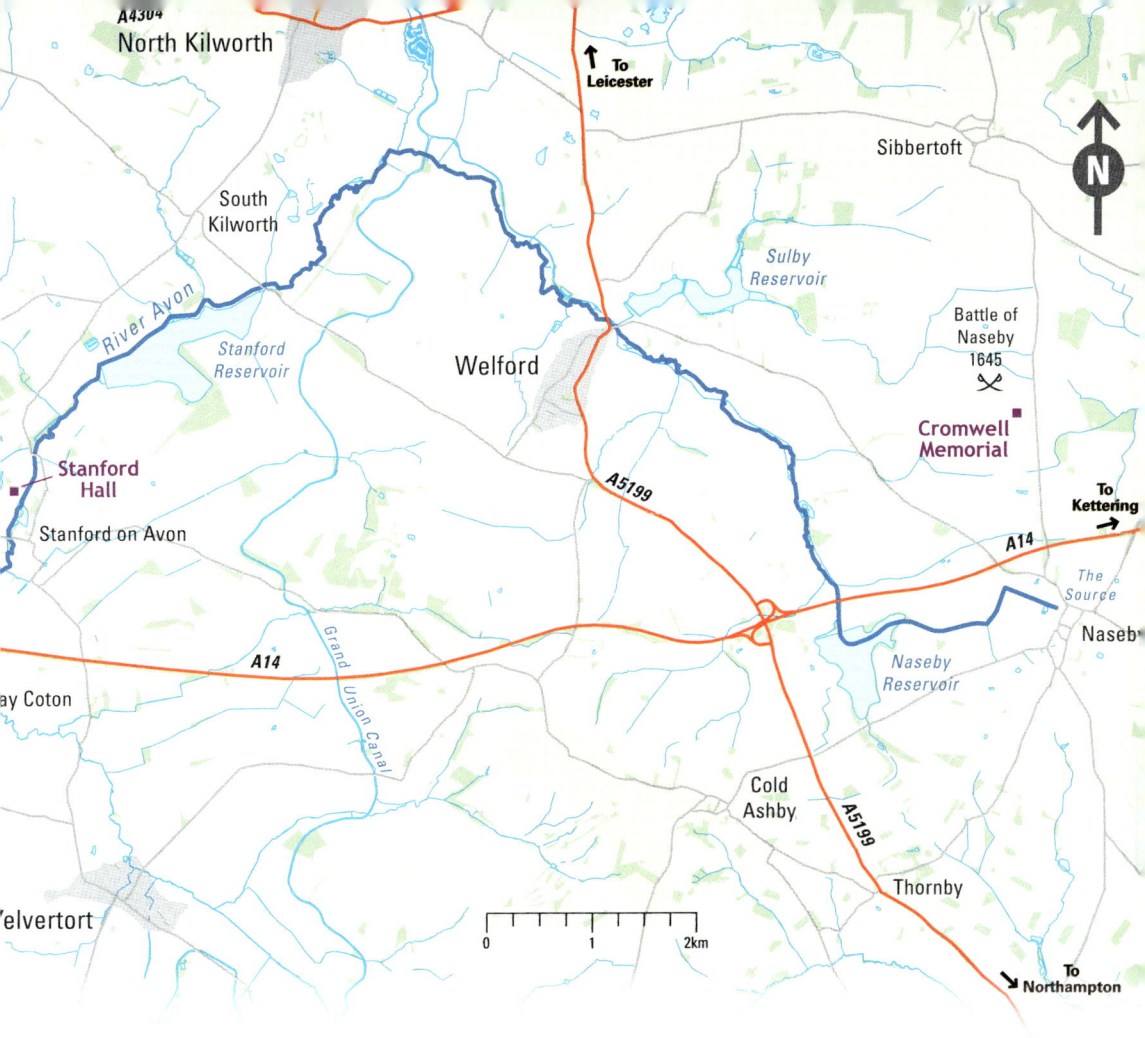

Avon's wiggling course now follows the border. At 13.7km, the Avon bypasses Stanford Reservoir along its northern edge. It then enters Stanford Park, being pooled by a weir into an ornamental lake fronting Stanford Hall. This seventeenth-century mansion and its grounds are open to the public on selected days. The pillar across the lake commemorates Lieutenant Percy Pilcher RN, the *'first man to fly in England'*. This little-known aviation pioneer died here in 1899; he aimed to demonstrate powered flight, four years ahead of the Wright Brothers. On the day his triplane failed to work, so instead Pilcher took to the air in his bird-like glider *Hawk* which broke apart and plunged to the ground.

Charles Showell enjoyed the Avon at Stanford Hall; *"the effect of the sunlight, broad shadows and autumnal tints, was truly enchanting"* (*Shakespeare's Avon, from source to Severn*, 1901). This is noteworthy as Showell was a misanthropist who denigrated pretty much everything that he encountered along the river! For example, he called Naseby, *"A very dead alive sort of place"*.

THE SOURCE

49

The Avon next passes beneath the M1. The motorway inescapably overshadows the motte and bailey earthworks at Lilbourne, but nevertheless this is an attractive spot. At 24.2km from the source, the river enters Warwickshire by passing beneath the A5 / Watling Street alongside the much older (1232) arches of Dow Bridge. It then reaches the town of Rugby. Rugby is not without interesting bits, most obviously the public school which, in 1823, invented a new sport when student William Webb Ellis, *'took the ball in his arms and ran with it'*, as a plaque at the school records (various Rugby experts dispute the veracity of this origin story). The Avon unfortunately bypasses these, passing largely unnoticed through a grim industrial park.

Variations

Certain (admirably certifiable) folk have attempted to paddle short sections of the Avon from at least as high as Stanford Reservoir.

Walking the source?
Walking the first 23km of the Shakespeare's Avon Way from the source to Rugby is a possible way of exploring the Avon. The surroundings are pleasant enough, but actually this stretch of the long-distance trail largely veers clear of the river and also includes some long, uninspiring, road sections. See page 39.

The Battle of Naseby
The decisive battle of the English Civil War took place on 14th June 1645, two kilometres north of Naseby. The highly disciplined Parliamentary New Model Army, led by Lord Fairfax and Oliver Cromwell, had a two to one advantage over the Royalist army, led by King Charles I and Prince Rupert. Charles had been reluctant to engage in battle, but after prolonged retreats felt compelled. The battle was a disaster for the Royalists; the King's army broke ranks and ran and Charles fled the battlefield, abandoning his personal papers. This was an additional catastrophe, for they proved his collusion with foreign powers; Parliament published them.

The battle is commemorated by an obelisk erected just north-east of Naseby in 1823, with a moralistic inscription: *'A USEFUL LESSON TO BRITISH KINGS NEVER TO EXCEED THE BOUNDS OF THEIR JUST PEROGATIVE'*. About 1.5km north of the village is the more evocative Cromwell Memorial (1936), overlooking the slopes where, *'Oliver Cromwell led the Cavalry charge which decided the issue of the battle and ultimately that of the great Civil War'*. Cromwell's body is rumoured to be buried on the battlefield (his head had a very different fate; Google it!).

Bushwhacking near the source. Photo | Dick Whitehouse.

"Smooth runs the water where the brook is deep ..."

... so says the Duke of Suffolk in *Henry VI, Part II*; a man who clearly formed his riverine views whilst strolling along the genteel banks of the Avon at Stratford. There is nothing smooth and nothing terribly deep about the Avon near its source; if I were you, I would stick to paddling the pretty bits. Why anyone would enter into combat with such a wild landscape, I cannot fathom ... and neither can my wife, fathom that is, my obsession with finding squiggly blue lines on OS maps and paddling a bathtub-shaped piece of plastic down them. So, what did we learn from our venture?

- Failure to get out after bog-hopping the stream along Stanford reservoir will drop you over a weir opposite the reservoir overflow and then down a concrete spillway.
- Below the reservoir is a completely wild landscape of fallen trees, long forgotten weirs, and the occasional stately home (Stanford Hall), followed by a few miles of spiky river gardening.
- Every so often, a helpful farmer will have gated the river.
- You can get out and admire a lovely motte and bailey at Lilbourne.
- None of the bridges are high enough for flood conditions; they'll probably find you in 300 years' time, when archaeologists excavate the A14.

On those happy notes, I wish you happy and safe paddling!

Dick Whitehouse

📷 *Near Long Lawford.*

Paddling through Newbold on Avon.

Section 1

The Upper Reaches

Distance 25.5km
Start △ Newbold on Avon SP 490 770 / CV21 1EF
Finish ◯ Bubbenhall SP 360 725 / CV8 3BE

Introduction

"By now, at seasons when the water table is up, the river has become canoeable."
Robert Aickman in *Portraits of Rivers*, 1953

The Avon is paddleable from Rugby, with much attractive countryside to enjoy. However, there are sharp variations in quality. The relatively short (13.7km) section recommended here will provide plenty of challenge and adventure.

Launch points

Newbold on Avon SP 490 770 / CV21 1EF – path on river right beside the bridge on Parkfield Road.

Bretford Bridge SP 429 769 / CV23 0LB – river left, above or below the bridge. Park across the bridge in Bretford and carry down.

Wolston SP 409 758 / CV8 3HP – either bank, a footbridge just downstream of the Main Street road bridge. Roadside parking nearby.

Citrus Hotel SP 368 753 / CV8 3DY – footpath on river left beside Ryton Bridge on the A45. The only parking is beside the motel, seek their permission.

Bubbenhall SP 360 725 / CV8 3BE – limited parking at the end of Church Road. Follow the footpath 270m through the church yard and along a field to a gate beside the river. River left.

Description
Newbold on Avon to Wolston 13.7km

"At Rugby our narrative, hitherto smilingly pastoral, quickens to epic. So far we had followed Avon afoot, but here we meant to launch a Canadian canoe on its waters."

Arthur Quiller-Couch,
The Warwickshire Avon, 1892

Quiller-Couch had the right idea; Rugby is the point from which to begin a paddling descent of the Avon, assuming you are prepared to accept a little tree-dodging. Choose a day when the river clearly has reasonable flow, but perhaps avoid mid-summer when it will be overgrown with reeds. Launching at the bridge in Newbold on Avon, the last vestiges of Rugby are quickly left behind. The first weir marked on the map is tiny and inconsequential, like all on this section.

After passing beneath an enormous railway viaduct and past the wastelands fronting Rugby Cement Works, things improve and you are rewarded with access to a hidden world of Warwickshire wilds. The river winds unhurriedly through open pastures past distant farm buildings, with only the grazing cows, sheep and horses to witness your passing. Occasionally it sinks from view beneath the farmland, passing through enclosing tunnels of trees. These often obscure the river at water level, and you will have to squeeze past many blockages and certainly portage several.

📷 *Railway bridge near Rugby.*

"The canoe darts in and out of rush beds; avoids now a shallow, now a snag, a clump of reeds, a conglomerate of logs ... and again is gliding easily between meadows."

Arthur Quiller-Couch,
The Warwickshire Avon, 1892

The going is slow (assume that the near-14km will take all day) and the landmarks are well-spaced. The former mill at Little Lawford is bypassed by a small weir channel. The first road bridge is encountered after 8.3km; if you choose to stretch your legs, just north along the road is King's Newnham Tower, an isolated remnant of a twelfth century church. Bretford Bridge, reached after 10.7km, is where the Roman Fosse Way (now the single-lane A428) crosses the river in five arches. The bridge replaced an ancient ford (the clue is in the name) and possibly dates from 1279. It was repaired in 1653, following Civil War damage. The Avon braids above and below the bridge and some channels are overgrown.

Your arrival at Wolston is heralded by a tall railway bridge, which you pass beneath. Take out at the road bridge and adjacent footbridge just downstream, 13.7km from the start. On river right are the earthworks of Brandon Castle; this was built in the twelfth century but demolished in 1265 during the Second Baronial War (see page 124).

Wolston to Bubbenhall 11.8km

Below Wolston, the frequency of tree blockages increases, until the river becomes impassable. After more than a dozen successive portages, the author abandoned the

 *Bretford Bridge.*

📷 *Above Wolston.*

river, exhausted and defeated, in the vicinity of Ryton-on-Dunsmore. The river continues to be overgrown past Brandon Marsh Nature Reserve (rewilded flooded gravel pits, on river right), before finally emerging beside a hotel at Ryton Bridge on the noisy A45 dual carriageway. The river is much less obstructed from here, and it is possible to launch for a 5.6km paddle to Bubbenhall. However, the Avon winds between unprepossessing horizons; Coventry Airport and Middlemarch Business Park (vast warehouses) to the north, and the Jaguar Land Rover plant to the south.

Guy's Cliffe House

Warwick Castle.

Section 2

Bubbenhall to Warwick

Distance 20.7km
Start △ Bubbenhall SP 360 725 / CV8 3BE
Finish ◯ St Nicholas Park SP 288 647 / CV34 4QY

Introduction

"It is not until it reaches Guy's Cliff, Warwick Castle and Charlecote Park that the winding Avon makes good its claim to beauty and picturesqueness"

Great Western Railway, *Shakespeare-Land, the World's Great Travel Shrine*, 1924

This superb trip follows the Avon's metamorphosis from reed-strewn stream into deep, wide (and stunningly beautiful) river. Several remarkable points of interest are encountered along the way including a stately home, a ghostly ruin and the spectacular finish below the walls of Warwick Castle.

The price of admission to this unique adventure is a degree of competence and experience in judging and paddling white water safely; six weirs add excitement and challenge, but are potentially dangerous and cannot be easily inspected or portaged.

Launch points

Bubbenhall SP 360 725 / CV8 3BE – limited parking at the end of Church Road. Follow the footpath 270m through the church yard and along a field to a gate beside the river.

Stare Bridge – SP 329 714 / CV8 2LH – a tiny

59

layby on the B4113 Stoneleigh Road. Carry your boat 200m along the footpath to the medieval bridge (not the modern road bridge). Ashow SP 311 702 / CV8 2LE – parking area at the end of Church Road. Follow the footpath through the churchyard. Awkward / difficult launch possible from the footpath on the river right downstream side of a footbridge.
Chesford Bridge SP 302 698 / CV8 2LN – parking for a couple of cars roadside. Launch from

Weir at Bubbenhall.

the footpath on river right, downstream of the bridge, down a steep overgrown bank. Not easy. Limited parking across the A452 on the B4115 lane, 200m uphill.

Hill Wootton Road SP 309 691 / CV32 6QN – parking for a couple of cars roadside, beside the bridge. Launch downstream of the bridge on river left.

St Nicholas Park SP 288 647 / CV34 4QY – a large car park across a public park from the river. Only a few spaces available without a height barrier.

Description

It should be obvious from the small size of the river, and from the quiet church yard where you start, that large or indiscreet groups would be inappropriate for this trip. Canadian canoes would also be a bad idea, due to the nature of the single definite portage. The river ideally needs flow from recent rain, but not so much as to make the weirs dangerous. A good gauge is the Bubbenhall start point, where you launch into the river left channel beside an old mill island. Don't head downstream, as this leads to a dangerous sluice. Paddle 50m upstream to where the water splits to flow over a miniature weir beneath a low footbridge. If there isn't space to comfortably duck under the footbridge, then you perhaps have too much water for the later weirs on this trip to be runnable.

The deceptively short distance to Bubbenhall Bridge is characterised by tortuous bends and several overgrown patches:

Cloud Bridge.

"The freakish stream went round and round, all meanders with never a forthright, narrowing, shallowing, casting up here a snag and there a thicket of reeds. And round and round for miles our canoe followed it, as a puppy chases his own tail; yet Bubbenhall was not, nor any glimpse of Bubbenhall ..."

Arthur Quiller-Couch,
The Warwickshire Avon, 1892

When the sandstone bridge is finally reached, the river widens and becomes less obstructed. Cloud Bridge follows shortly after, another attractive sandstone edifice. The name comes from the Old English *clude*: a rocky spot. Passing beneath Cloud Bridge, you enter Stoneleigh Deer Park. This is an idyllic vale, with old oaks dotting the slopes of Motslow Hill on river right.

"The river meanders with a genial murmur through fertile meads, between banks, at one point so steep that the ripple from the faintest breeze washes over the daisies that bedeck them"

James Thorne,
Rambles by Rivers: The Avon, 1845

The park, now a golf course, is a remnant of the Forest of Arden, Shakespeare's *"uncouth forest"* which once stretched as far as Staffordshire and was the semi-mythical setting for *A Midsummer Night's Dream* and *As You Like It*. *"I like this place and could willingly waste my time in it"*. You pass beneath two footbridges within the park, the second leading into a relatively friendly (but walled-in) sloping weir. There are two Stare Bridges; the newer (1929) three-arched bridge carries the Stoneleigh Road; the medieval Stare Bridge is directly

Weir above Stare Bridge.

afterwards, and is unmistakeable with its nine arches. Over the next four kilometres, the Avon describes a big loop around Stoneleigh Park, a huge agricultural and events complex. The only hint of this is a series of gated footbridges. However, the controversial HS2 rail link which is due for completion in 2026 will certainly be conspicuous, as it will pass through Stoneleigh Park, paralleling the Avon north-west from Stare Bridge before crossing near the River Sowe confluence. At the time of writing, extensive local woodlands have already been obliterated in scorched-earth preparation for this obscenely expensive vanity project, of questionable necessity.

"The size of Avon is almost doubled by junction with the Sowe, a stream that comes winding past Stoneleigh village on our right, and brings for tribute the impurities of Coventry ..."

Arthur Quiller-Couch,
The Warwickshire Avon, 1892

Quiller-Couch's description is accurate about the widening of the Avon, and quite possibly also about the water quality.

The scenery changes to the landscaped parkland around Stoneleigh Abbey:

Stoneleigh Deer Park.

"Stoneleigh Abbey is most delightfully situated in the midst of a luxuriant and fertile country, adorned by extensive and venerable woods, and watered by the Avon, which being here of ample breadth, flows through the grounds with a noble effect. Over one part of this river is a fine Bridge, of one arch, erected from a plan of Mr Rennie."

Francis Smith, *An Historical and Descriptive Guide to Leamington Spa*, 1827

The balustraded New Bridge was designed in 1814 by engineer John Rennie (of Bell Rock lighthouse and Waterloo Bridge fame). In 1848, estate owner Chandos Leigh underwent trial for murder of two stonemasons who were alleged to have been crushed, on his orders, during the bridge's construction. The charge was thrown out, but stories persist that their bodies remain within the stonework.

The river splits; avoid the river left channel which leads eventually to an unwelcoming tunnel-sluice and instead descend the sloping weir to join the river right channel. Avoid this walled-in weir in high water, when the stopper is potentially grabby. The river right channel leads to an awkward obstacle; a 'bailey' bridge (a prefab design from WWII) which crosses at river level. There isn't space to squeeze beneath, therefore the solution is to unobtrusively portage across the bridge, through the trusses on the river left side; a Canadian canoe will not fit. This activity would be inappropriate with a large or disorganised group.

Directly downstream Stoneleigh Abbey, an enormous Georgian mansion, watches over the pooled waters where the two channels reconverge. This artificial 'mirror lake' is

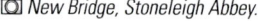
New Bridge, Stoneleigh Abbey.

📷 *Weir below Stoneleigh Abbey.*

created by a weir 300m past the house, which drops steeply away but seems forgiving. The lake was temporarily filled during the Second World War after German bombers used it as a waypoint to locate Coventry.

The Avon flows swiftly for the two kilometres to Ashow, where a stone bench on river right below the church makes for an idyllic lunch

📷 *Rail viaduct before Saxon Mill.*

spot. The A452 crosses at Chesford Bridge; this was formerly the 'Welsh Road', the cattle drovers' route to the South East. Kenilworth, with its spectacular ruined castle, is just a short distance north-west along the road. The former Blackdown Mill (now an antiques dealer) is passed on river left beside the following bridge. The banks then open out so that the long, high railway viaduct which crosses the valley makes quite an impression.

The Avon now swings south in front of Blacklow Hill. The hill is notable for Gaveston's Cross, an 1832 memorial: *'In the hollow of this rock was beheaded by barons as lawless as himself, Piers Gaveston, Earl of Cornwall, the minion of a hateful king'.* Gaveston was executed in 1312 due to his Rasputin-like influence over Edward II. Sadly, visiting it up close now

Stoneleigh Abbey

Stoneleigh Abbey was a Cistercian monastery from 1154. After Henry VIII dissolved the monasteries in the 1530s, the Leigh family acquired the lands. The current baroque house dates from between 1714 and 1726, and the 279 hectares of parkland (including damming the Avon to create the 'mirror lake' before the house) were landscaped by Humphry Repton in the late eighteenth century. Jane Austen visited in 1806, and Stoneleigh Abbey makes an appearance as 'Sotherton Court' in *Northanger Abbey*. Other visitors have included Queen Victoria and Prince Albert.

The Leighs passed the estate to a charitable trust in 1996 and the house is now open to the public. It was renovated with public money; awkwardly, some of the original £10 million Heritage Lottery Fund and English Heritage grants were shown to have been siphoned off for property investments and to pay debts. The trust has since been under new management.

involves a death-defying crossing of the A46. As the Avon approaches Warwick (river right) and Royal Leamington Spa (river left), it still holds a few treats. Picturesque Saxon Mill (now a pub) sits alongside a footbridge and weir, the latter being a straightforward ledge drop. There had already been a mill here for at least two centuries when it was mentioned in the 1086 Domesday Book. Ruskin painted this lovely spot and antiquarian William Camden

Saxon Mill.

📷 *Guy's Cliffe House.*

seems to have appreciated it: *"A shady little wood, cleere and cristal springs, mossie bottoms and caves, medowes alwaies fresh and greene, the river rumbling heere and there among the stones"* (*Britannia*, 1586).

The caves that Camden mentioned are directly downstream, where the Avon bends left beneath sandstone cliffs. Guy's Cave is one of a series scoured out of the rock; Guy of Warwick was a mythical knight and hermit popularised in twelfth-century romance tales; he slayed the Dun Cow monster which terrorised the locale, and his wife Felice took her life by jumping into the river here. The astonishing ruin towering atop the cliffs is Guy's Cliffe House. This is the ghostly shell of a 1751 Georgian mansion, abandoned after 1946 and accidentally burned in 1992 during filming of a Sherlock Holmes story. Landing to explore (on the beach beside Guy's Church, just downstream) is discouraged.

"Trees droop densely over the soft water; the house itself is late Gothic; there are a mill, an ancient chapel with a huge rock statue and an eremitical cave: and all, needless to say, are in the last stages of decay."

Robert Aickman in *Portraits of Rivers* 1953 You probably knew this, but 'eremitical' means: to do with hermits.

The final few kilometres pass right through the two towns, yet remain green and unsullied, with parkland along the banks. Two adjacent weirs give access to a river right channel; paddle the first, which is sloping and user-friendly. The A445 bridge leads to the confluence of the River Leam on river left, then the Grand

◎ *The Old Castle Bridge, Warwick.*

Union Canal aqueduct and a railway bridge are passed under in quick succession, before reaching St Nicholas Park. You'll blink and do a double-take, but don't adjust your glasses; you really *are* seeing pink flamingo pedalos.

The trip is over, but you will absolutely want to paddle a short distance further, past Castle Bridge, to take in the amazing sight of the sheer walls and towers of Warwick Castle, rearing above the Avon.

"and suddenly, by the famous onespan bridge, see Warwick Castle full ahead, its massy foundations growing, as it seems, from the living rock, and Caesar's glorious tower soaring above ... We turn our canoe, and with many a backward look paddle back."

Arthur Quiller-Couch,
The Warwickshire Avon, 1892

Variations

The village of Stoneleigh can be visited by following the River Sowe for 1km upstream from the Avon.

The River Leam gives access to Royal Leamington Spa (Nathaniel Hawthorne: *"One of the cosiest nooks in England or in the world"*) and its centrepiece attractions. 900m upstream

◎ *Warwick.*

from the confluence, portage around a weir via a path on river right. Two kilometres from the Avon you reach the Royal Pump Room Gardens, in the heart of the Georgian town. Leamington was known, from the fifteenth century, for its saline springs. The Regency craze for spa cures saw the town balloon into a resort (population: 315 in 1801, 13,000 in 1841). The Pump Room was opened by local doctor Henry Jepson in 1814, visitors included Charles Dickens (who set *Dombey and Son* here) and the future Queen Victoria and her mother. Victoria granted the Royal Charter in 1838 (26 days after her coronation), making Leamington the world's first 'Royal' town.

Caesar's Tower, Warwick Castle.

Warwick Castle

Warwick Castle originated in around 914 when Æthelflæd (King Alfred's daughter and Lady of the Mercians) built a fort on a rocky prominence above the Avon, to defend against the Danes. Following the Norman Conquest, in 1068 a motte and bailey castle was constructed, later rebuilt in stone. The castle expanded to its current massive scale under seven generations of the Beauchamp family, who in the fourteenth century added the imposing Guy's and Caesar's Towers. After the death of the rebellious Warwick the Kingmaker in 1471, the castle passed to the crown. Elizabeth I granted it to Ambrose Dudley (brother of her 'favourite' Robert Dudley, who owned nearby Kenilworth Castle). In 1604 it was acquired by the Grevilles, who converted it to a stately home. The vast wall overshadowing the Avon is the main residence, with five state rooms. In the eighteenth century, Lancelot 'Capability' Brown remodelled the grounds, and Warwick's West Street Bridge was demolished to give a 'Romantic' effect. Merlin Entertainments (owners of Alton Towers) have owned the castle since 2007 and have developed it into a theme park-style attraction. This is not everyone's cup of tea, but just tune out the 'ye olde worlde' nonsense and marvel at this incredible monumental fortress which has endured on the banks of the Avon.

Warwick Castle.

Leaford Bridge.

Section 3

Warwick to Stratford-upon-Avon

Distance 23.3km
Start △ St Nicholas Park SP 288 647 / CV34 4QY
Finish ○ Recreation Ground, Stratford-upon-Avon SP 204 546 / CV37 7PY

Introduction

"From Warwick to Stratford, where the Avon has never been harnessed (except by mills) is the stretch I love best. It is only fourteen miles, but fourteen miles of clear, quick water, running in scours between wooded sloping meadows."

William Bliss,
The Heart of England by Waterway, 1933

A favourite of pioneering paddler William Bliss, no further recommendation is needed! His description still fully applies; also factor in Warwick Castle, glorious Charlecote Park and arrival at bustling Stratford-upon-Avon, and you have one of the finest British paddle trips.

Launch points

St Nicholas Park SP 288 647 / CV34 4QY – a large car park across a public park from the river. Only a few spaces available without a height barrier.

Barford SP 267 609/ CV35 8EH – Barford Bridge (the old bridge), accessed from Hewitt Road. Park in the village. The river can also be accessed from the junction of Keyte's Lane and Carter Drive.

Hampton Lucy SP 257 571 / CV35 8BA – an awkward scramble from the bridleway track on river right, upstream of the bridge.

Alveston SP 236 565 / CV37 7QX – river left.

Follow the footpath from the end of Ferry Lane, past houses and then down steps to the river. Park near the Ferry Inn.

Tiddington SP 220 560 / CV37 7AN – follow the path continuing from the end of School Lane.

Park in the village. Obscured by trees and hard to spot from the water.

The Old Bathing Place SP 209 557 / CV37 0NS – large free riverside car park on the A439 Warwick Road. Stupidly, it has a height barrier.

◎ *St Nicholas Park, Warwick.*

Stratford-upon-Avon (Recreation Ground) SP 204 546 / CV37 7PY – Recreation Ground car park on river left across the river from the Royal Shakespeare Theatre, 300m past Clopton Bridge. Expensive.

Description

The first kilometre of this trip needs the most thought. Warwick Castle is owned by Merlin Entertainments, the theme park entertainment company, who – obviously – have zero jurisdiction over how people might enjoy Britain's rivers. However, two factors complicate things; firstly the weir beside the castle is one of the less inviting ones on the Avon and usually needs to be portaged, and secondly the parkland on both banks of the river directly below is actively used for faux-medieval entertainments watched by crowds of tourists, meaning that you might disturb these (and risk getting an arrow in your head!). There is currently only one viable solution; time your launch to pass the castle at the earliest possible hour, literally at or before dawn, and pass through quickly. If you are not an early bird, Barford is the place to start.

Castle Bridge was constructed in 1793 for George Greville, 2nd Earl of Warwick, from sandstone brought downriver from Emscote. The fourteen-arch medieval bridge 250m downstream beside the castle was demolished and Castle Street, Warwick's main thoroughfare, was walled off to exclude the unwashed public from his proximity, and to create a garden. Parts of the old bridge were left in place as a romantic ruin, and to be fair it does make for a fine sight.

Castle Bridge, Warwick.

"The eye is gratified with an extensive view of Warwick town, the venerable castle, and the new bridge recently built by the Earl of Warwick. Our Avon, gently winding through the extensive meadows before us, passes under this elegant and simple arch, through the highly ornamented grounds of its noble owner."

Samuel Ireland, *Picturesque Views on the Upper, or Warwickshire Avon*, 1795

Warwick aptly means, *'dwelling by weir'*. The weir is hard to overlook, as two successive cables are slung across the river carrying warning signs. Paddle past the two small channels leading off on river left (the first to a sluice and the second to a vertical weir) to the island on river left above the main weir. The main weir drops steeply and can produce a notable towback at higher levels. It is possible to discreetly portage around the main weir across this river left island. The island long ago housed a menagerie of exotic animals – thankfully nowadays it's uninhabited!

In the pool below, you enjoy a truly privileged view of the castle. A mill and enormous waterwheel jut into the river right side of the weir; this was converted to power 474 light bulbs in 1894, and has been restored to working order. Caesar's Tower (built 1330–60) towers above the mill, encircled by crenulations. Monolithic walls follow the river to Watergate Tower, also known as the Ghost Tower; supposedly haunted by Earl of Warwick Sir Fulke Greville, who was stabbed by a servant in 1628, over a pay dispute. Past this you get a view of the Castle Mound, the site of the original fortification built to defend against the Vikings.

The gardens on both banks past the castle are adorned with tourism paraphernalia, including a trebuchet and archery targets, followed by the tents of a holiday resort. The Avon then flows through the quiet grounds of Castle Park.

"A mile and a half of natural beauty which has been enhanced and not spoiled by man ... it is truly a beautiful place; the great trees have been well planted, and the open park is closed in and set about with woods ... the Avon takes on something of the character of an ornamental water."

William Bliss,
The Heart of England by Waterway 1933

The river pools up, despite the lack of a retaining weir. The widest point is at a right bend passing the mouth of New Waters, an artificial lake engineered for Francis Greville, the 1st Earl of Warwick. He is also responsible for Leafield Bridge (1775) which crosses the river from the hillside of Lodge Wood to approach the castle.

"We could not fail to notice the splendid scenery through which we were passing. The river was wide and very deep, not a weed to be seen; the water was almost black, with no perceptible current. On either side were high hills covered down to the water's edge with the most magnificent foliage."

Howard Williams, *The Diary of a Rowing Tour from Oxford to London*, 1875

The M40 River Avon Bridge (two parallel bridges) is a jarring return to the modern world, although it is actually relatively unobtrusive. The boathouse of the University of Warwick Rowing Club is below on river right,

Castle Park.

Below Barford Weir.

be alert for rowers in the kilometre down to Barford Weir. Here, the water drops onto a sill into a river right channel, before ducking into a tree-lined tunnel which is sometimes blocked by wood debris.

Howard Williams's rowing crew became pinned and spent an afternoon hauling their scull off a tree:

"The river ran so swiftly that at times it was impossible to guide the boat, and it was so narrow and tortuous that we constantly stuck in the bushes, and often ran aground."

Howard Williams, *The Diary of a Rowing Tour from Oxford to London*, 1875

When the Avon re-joins its river-left channel, Barford comes into view on river left; you will spot a small lane which gives access to the river, and then you reach Barford's eighteenth-century bridge, crossing at a shallow point (Williams became stuck here, also). Along the road on river left is The Joseph Arch, a pub named for Barford's most famous son. Arch founded the National Agricultural Workers Union in 1872 and was, in 1885, the first agricultural worker to become an MP. His grave is in the churchyard.

Barford Weir.

Barford is bypassed by a new (2007) bridge carrying the A429, and then the Avon commences a winding eight-kilometre stretch to Hampton Lucy. William Bliss described, *"stickles and scours all the way for the next three miles till you begin to feel the hold-up of the next mill at Hampton Lucy"* (*The Heart of England by Waterway*, 1933).

The main landmark is the spire of All Saints Church, designed in 1862–4 by Sir Gilbert Scott (who also restored churches at Wasperton and Hampton Lucy), viewed from all directions! *"So many and abrupt are these bends that the slim spire of Sherborne across the meadows appeared now to right, now to left; now dodged behind us, now stood up straight ahead."*

Arthur Quiller-Couch,
The Warwickshire Avon, 1892

Barford Bridge.

The village of Wasperton is seen across the fields on river left, before the river is forced south by 86m Copdock Hill, following the steep and wooded Scar Bank. Look out for a damaged aircraft propellor mounted on the river right bank, a memorial, *'TO THE MEMORY OF THE TWO COMMONWEALTH AIR CREWS WHO DIED ON THIS STRETCH OF RIVER 1942*

Barford.

Hampton Lucy Weir.

AND 1943 – LEST WE FORGET'. Ten men lost their lives in crashes here.

The tower of St Peter's Church (1826) signifies that you've reached Hampton Lucy. The river left channel which continues ahead is blocked by lovely Charlecote Mill, an eighteenth-century redbrick building which was restored in 1978 and now grinds corn again (and is sometimes open to visitors). Hampton Lucy Weir slides into the river right channel via a moderately sticky stopper. Portaging on river right is easy. Below the weir, a winding channel leads down to a cast iron bridge which was built in 1829 at Horseley Iron Works at Ironbridge in Shropshire.

A floating barrier signifies that you've reached the National Trust property of Charlecote Park. It's not too tricky to push past the cable, but this deer barrier has historically been a bugbear for river users. Thankfully the wall of posts and planks encountered by Howard Williams no longer exists: *"... altogether we considered ourselves lucky in getting across"* (*The Diary of a Rowing Tour from Oxford to London*, 1875). Charlecote Park, ranged along the river left bank, is quite a sight. 75 hectares of landscaped

Charlecote Park.

📷 *Charlecote Park.*

Charlecote Park

"Charlecote Park is the park of the Shakespeare deer-poaching legend and is, in its way, even more beautiful than Warwick Park."

William Bliss,

The Heart of England by Waterway 1933

Bliss is referring to a story that a young William Shakespeare was caught poaching deer in the park and as a result had to leave for London; hence launching his literary career. Factual evidence supporting this is pretty tenuous, revolving around several well-informed hunting references in his plays.

*"What, hast not thou full often struck a doe
And borne her cleanly by the keeper's nose?"*

Titus Andronicus

The Lucy family have resided here since 1274, presenting the park to the National Trust in 1946. The mansion was built c1558 (replacing a moated medieval manor) in the shape of the letter 'E', to honour Elizabeth I. However, its current Jacobean appearance is largely due to nineteenth century rebuilding. Charlecote Park was landscaped by Lancelot 'Capability' Brown in 1760. A visit is recommended, the entrance and the car park are in the village of Charlecote. Arrivals by kayak (NT members or not!) would possibly be frowned upon?

River Dene confluence, Charlecote Park.

deer park surround a sixteenth-century mansion, directly overlooking the water. Below the mansion, the River Dene tumbles into the Avon via an ornamental waterfall, and then a second deer barrier marks the exit from the park.

The final challenge of the day comes shortly after the village of Alveston. Overlooked by Alveston House (1689), tiny Alveston Weir

Alveston Weir.

leads into a river right channel. The subsequent jungly section is described by Charles Showell as, *"one of the most secluded places on the river"* (Shakespeare's Avon, from source to Severn, 1901), winding some distance away from the main channel.

"... very beautiful scenery, which changed in feature every few minutes; one minute we went along water that was as wide as the Thames, and the next found us in what was more like a brook, with the trees almost meeting above our heads and the stream rushing under us and carrying us along at a tremendous pace around sharp corners."

Howard Williams, *The Diary of a Rowing Tour from Oxford to London*, 1875

Alveston Weir is the upstream limit of the Avon Navigation, but it's a couple more kilometres, passing Hatton Rock cliff on river right, before

Royal Shakespeare Theatre.

you reach the sharp right bend at Avoncliffe, where the river becomes safe for larger craft. All that remains is to paddle past the gardens of Tiddington and through a large holiday park (on both banks joined by a footbridge), overlooked on river right by the 37m obelisk atop Potato Hill, highest of the Welcombe Hills. Take out on river right at The Old Bathing Place, or continue a further kilometre to the busy madness of Stratford, passing beneath Clopton Bridge and the Tramway Bridge to finish opposite the Royal Shakespeare Theatre.

Variations

Royal Leamington Spa Canoe Club organise an annual charity paddle along this section, known as the Doggy Paddle. As there is support and safety cover at the weirs, this is a great way for the less confident to experience this outstanding journey.

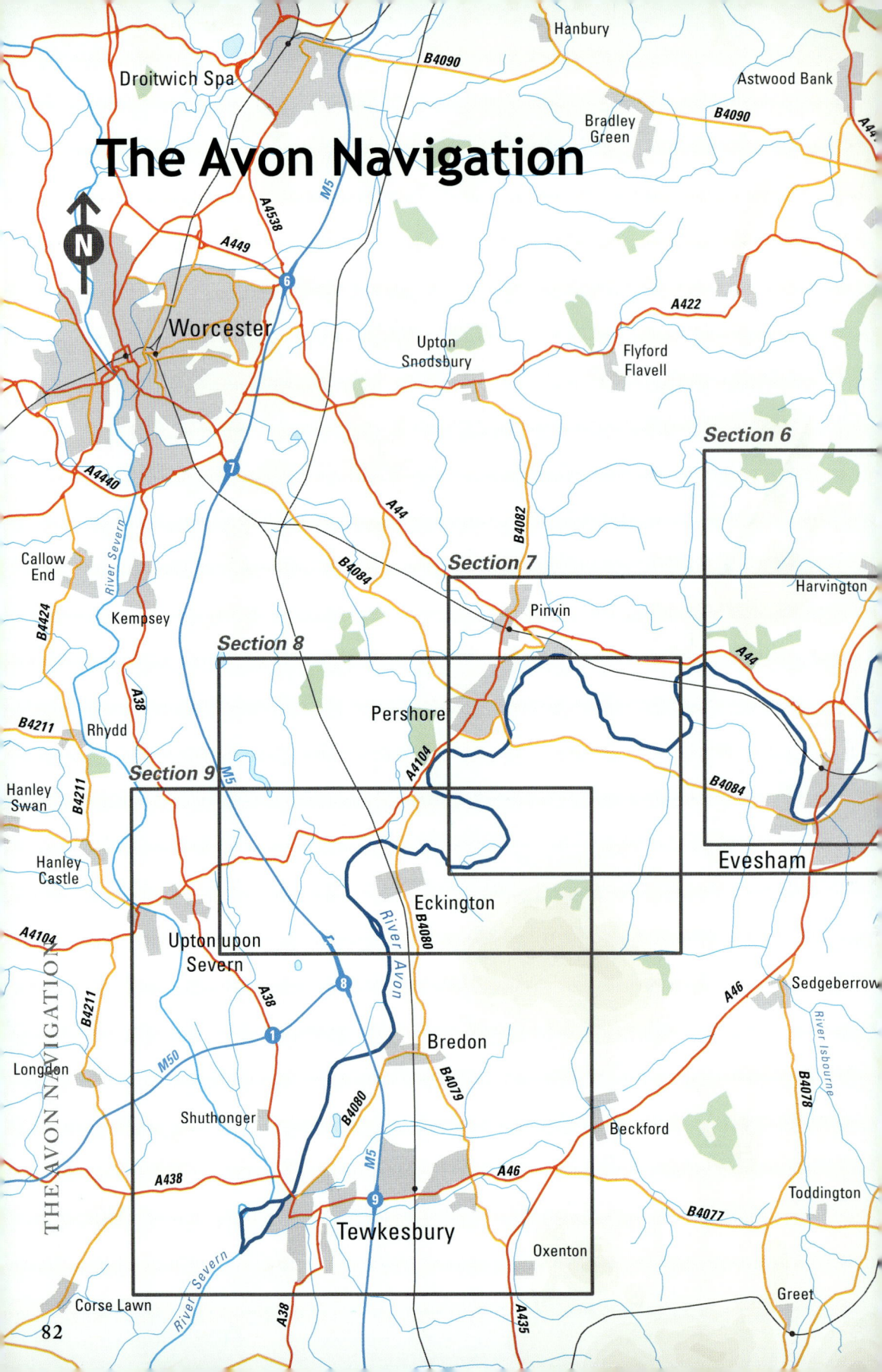

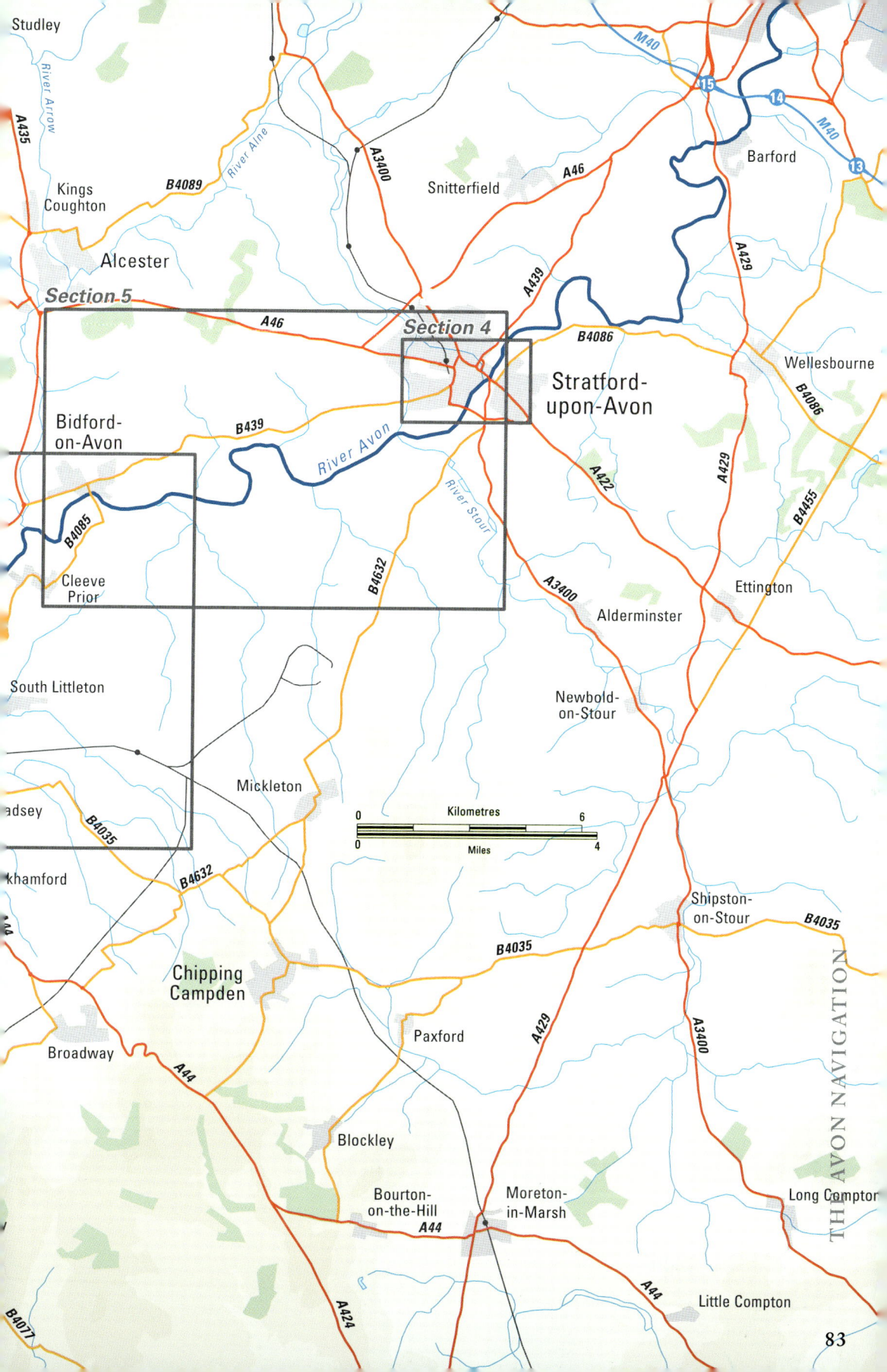

Lucy's Mill Weir.

Clopton Bridge.

Section 4

Stratford-upon-Avon

Distance 2.2km
Start △ Recreation Ground, Stratford-upon-Avon SP 204 546 / CV37 7PY
Finish ◯ Recreation Ground, Stratford-upon-Avon SP 204 546 / CV37 7PY

Introduction

"The river adds greatly to the pleasure of life at Stratford. It is a beautiful stream, which it is a delight to look upon and float upon, and to study."

John Henry Garrett, *The Idyllic Avon*, 1906

Outlined here is the mere 1.1km stretch of the Avon between Stratford-upon-Avon's two road bridges. This is a pleasant spot to launch, potter about and explore, with plenty of interest along or near the waterfront ... much of it, of course, being Shakespeare-related. There is also a bit of white-water interest, for those so inclined. The river provides the closest thing in Stratford to a peaceful haven, offering distance from its hordes of tourists. That said, after a morning spent enjoying Stratford from the water you really should venture ashore for a spot of sightseeing ...

Launch points

Stratford-upon-Avon (Recreation Ground) SP 204 546 / CV37 7PY – Recreation Ground car park on river left across the river from the Royal Shakespeare Theatre, 300m past Clopton Bridge. Expensive.

Description

The Avon at Stratford is always busy with hired rowing boats, punts and canoes. Keep an eye out also for training rowing boats. The river and its banks will be particularly crammed during the Stratford River Festival (held over two days in July) and you may also wish to be aware of the annual Mop Fair, which has been held in October since the seventeenth century.

Launching from the Recreation Ground car park will locate you directly in front of / opposite the Royal Shakespeare Theatre. This is 300m downstream of Clopton Bridge, Stratford's central road crossing. The river is described here from the bridge downstream, so start off by paddling up to and beneath it.

Directly upstream of Clopton Bridge on river right are a number of side channels, occupied by moored boats. Hidden at the back of these (and overlooked by the Crowne Plaza Hotel) is the Avon Swan Reserve, a quiet backwater. By the 1980s, poisoning by angler's lead weights had caused the town's swan population to crash to a single pair. Mindful that Shakespeare was known as, *"the Sweet Swan of Avon"*, the mayor set up the reserve. There are now over thirty pairs and the birds are once more a ubiquitous feature of Stratford's waters.

"Afore the time of Hugh Clopton there was but a poor bridge of timber, and no causeway to come to it, whereby many poor folks either refused to come to Stratford when the river was up, or coming thither stood in jeopardy of life"

John Leland, *The Itinerary* 1535-43

Clopton was a Stratford local who, like Shakespeare, made his fortune in the capital,

◉ *Tramway Bridge.*

becoming Lord Mayor of London in 1491. He remembered his roots by funding the bridge's construction, c1486. It was originally 335m long but floods destroyed both ends in 1588, Parliamentary forces demolished an arch during the Civil War in 1643 and it was widened in 1814, with a tollhouse added on river right. Clopton Bridge survives today as a 150m-long structure comprising of fourteen pointed arches, supporting a perpetual traffic jam.

Directly downstream of Clopton Bridge on river right is a former timber yard with a distinctive tall redbrick chimney, now Cox's Yard restaurant. On the opposite shore are the Swan's Nest Hotel (another redbrick building, opened in 1662 as The Bear) and Avon Boating who, since 1895, have been hiring out watercraft from canoes and punts to gondolas and gin cruisers. These establishments are all boxed in by the Tramway Bridge, Stratford's second central crossing. This was built in 1823 to carry the Stratford and Moreton Horse Tramway; on river right in Bancroft Basin there is a preserved horse-drawn truck on a section of plateway. Nowadays Tramway Bridge is a busy footpath and also part of National Cycle Route 41.

The river left bank below Tramway Bridge is occupied by the Stratford Big Wheel (the Midlands' answer to the London Eye) and other tourist attractions, followed by the green spaces of the Recreation Ground (backed by the car park), extending downstream as far as Stratford Trinity Lock.

"The river-front of Stratford, the Clopton Bridge and the running Avon are obstinately beautiful."

John Russell, *Shakespeare's Country* 1942

◉ *Avon at Stratford.*

Exploring the river right bank of the Avon below the bridges makes for a fine introductory tour of Stratford's heritage and Shakespearean links. The lock gates alongside the Tramway Bridge are the entrance to Bancroft Basin, also known as Stratford Canal Basin. After years of dereliction, the restored lock and canal were reopened in 1964 by the Queen Mother, who passed through in a canal barge! The *William James* is moored in the basin, a long white canal barge which serves as the Stratford Waterways Information Centre, run by both the Canal & River Trust and Avon Navigation Trust. Licenses for the Avon can be acquired here.

Bancroft Basin is surrounded by Bancroft Gardens, the town's bustling social centre. Formerly, this was an industrial site with warehouses and tramway sidings; the gardens also occupy a second canal basin, filled in 1901. Consider landing here (negotiating through hire boats and vociferous swans) to engage with this chaotic cultural hub; international tourists sunbathe among various sculptures, artistic exhibits and performance spaces (and the occasional living statue, 'Shakespeare's Ghost' being a personal favourite). Across the canal basin is the Gower Monument, commissioned by Lord Ronald Sutherland Gower and sculpted in 1888. Shakespeare sits atop a plinth, brooding in bronze and smeared with pigeon shit. He is surrounded by statues respectively representing four themes of his plays: Lady Macbeth (Tragedy), Hamlet (Philosophy), Prince Hal (History) and Falstaff (Comedy).

Presiding over this whole scene and dominating the Avon's bank for over a hundred metres is the remarkable Royal Shakespeare Theatre.

It is, apparently, a classic of Modernist design. The author knows nothing about architecture, but can say with confidence that it looks as if it was designed by a particularly dysfunctional committee, with a whole range of contrasting and even clashing styles heaped together ... to surprisingly pleasing effect. This iconic redbrick edifice was designed by Elizabeth Scott and opened by the future King Edward VIII on 23rd April 1932, Shakespeare's 368th birthday (and 316th death-day). It replaced the Shakespeare Memorial Theatre, which opened in 1879 but burned down in 1926 (despite the river's proximity). In 1961 the theatre acquired the 'Royal' appellation and in 2010 it reopened after a £113 million refit, which included adding the 33m tower. The curved downstream end of the building is the Swan Theatre, opened in 1986 by Queen Elizabeth II. Avonbank Park, the strip of riverside greenery after the theatres, has an outdoor stage, The Dell. Free public performances take place in the summer months; check the RSC's schedule beforehand and you could combine paddling and high culture!

All of this, and now you get to encounter the Bard of Avon himself. Well, nearly; he's located a short distance further along the river right bank, buried in the chancel of Holy Trinity Church, where he was also baptised. Originating in 1210, this Cotswold stone church is the oldest building in Stratford. It's possible to land outside the church grounds and visit (perhaps ditch your dripping paddling kit at the gate). In return for a donation, you can enter the most visited parish church in

[◎] *Royal Shakespeare Theatre.*

📷 *Stratford Trinity Lock.*

England and view the Shakespeare Funerary Monument (c1623) with its life-size bust and Shakespeare's grave, alongside that of his wife Anne Hathaway. Shakespeare's gravestone bears his famous warning,

"Blest be ye man yt spares thes stones,
And curst be he yt moves my bones".

The river just downstream from the church is barred by a fairly impenetrable floating barrier, intended to prevent tourists in hire boats from descending Stratford's two weirs*. This means that you are forced to get out and portage around **Stratford Trinity Lock**, located to river left. Also known as Colin P. Witter Lock, this can be portaged on either side, with landing stages on river left above the lock and river right below. The lock was opened by the Queen in 1974, having been constructed through voluntary labour by inmates from Gloucester Gaol. It was possibly the hardest to build on the river, as the ground was insecure and silty; the eventual solution was the unusual steel 'box' that you see today. The former Lucy's Locks, a two-stage affair, are buried under a mound on river left.

Below the lock, the river is notably quieter. It is a simple 250m paddle to Lucy's Mill Bridge, if you are heading on downstream. However, most paddlers linger around this spot, to play or just explore. A chain of islands stretches diagonally across the Avon from the lock, joined by the two Lucy's Mill Weirs. The first weir

---

*The barrier must have been less substantial back when a teenage incarnation of the author floated past and unwisely descended the weirs in a tiny inflatable dinghy.

Lucy's Mill Weir.

rail bridge for Stratford and Midland Junction Railway; this closed in the 1960s.

If you are just here to enjoy Stratford, now is the point to turn about and paddle back upstream to the lock. If you decide to pass beneath the bridges and continue downstream, you immediately access an entirely different environment and adventure ...

is a staircase design, with uninviting rocks visible at the base. The second is sloping and is a popular playspot at low levels; an eddy queue of white-water paddlers can regularly be found here on weekend mornings. The occasional canoe slalom event is still held at the weirs (the author won a novice category event here in the 1980s, and has never stopped banging on about it since).

Lucy's Mill is long gone, but the river right site is occupied by flats whose design vaguely recalls a mill building. Below are two adjacent bridges; Lucy's Mill Bridge is a footbridge erected in 1934 on the site of a wooden bridge from c1599, and the arched road bridge below carries the A4390. The latter was formerly a

Variations

The Stratford-upon-Avon Canal can be explored up from Bancroft Basin, although there is nothing of special interest along the section through town. Paddlers thinking bigger will want to be aware of the 'Avon Ring'; the canal leads 41km north to the Worcester and Birmingham Canal, via 52 locks (also connecting to the Grand Union Canal at Kingswood Junction). From Birmingham, the Worcester and Birmingham Canal leads to the River Severn, which of course has its confluence with the Avon at Tewkesbury. William Bliss completed this 175km expedition, and has some advice: *"I remind canoeists as to plan any tour that takes in Avon that they go down it and not up"* (*Canoeing*, 1934).

Marie Corelli

One of the more peculiar sights the Avon has witnessed was an authentic Venetian gondola (complete with authentic Venetian gondolier), in which novelist Mary Mackay (1855-1924) would be ferried up and down-river. Better known by her pseudonym Marie Corelli, she relocated to Stratford after bestselling success and (despite extensive mockery for the gondola eccentricity) was instrumental in campaigning and fundraising for the preservation of the town's historic buildings. Her original gondola can sometimes be seen on the river; it was fully restored and now belongs to Avon Boating.

Stratford-upon-Avon and Shakespeare

*"Sweet Swan of Avon! What a sight it were
To see thee in our waters yet appear,
And make those flights upon the banks of Thames
That so did take Eliza, and our James!"*
Ben Jonson, *To the Memory of My Beloved, the Author, Mr. William Shakespeare*, in the preface to the *First Folio* of Shakespeare's plays, 1623

Neither Stratford or the Avon were mentioned in Shakespeare's plays or poems, and much of his life and work played out in London. Nevertheless, Shakespeare and Stratford have become inextricably linked. Stratford (originally *Stretford*; street-ford) was a settlement since at least the Bronze Age, but grew into a town after the granting of a market in 1124. It was controlled by The Guild of the Holy Cross (a religious order) until the dissolution of the monasteries, when their properties were all closed except for the Guild Chapel School. Shakespeare attended this between 1571 (aged seven) and 1578, and possibly didn't enjoy his education ...

*"... the whining schoolboy, with his satchel
And shining morning face, creeping like a snail
Unwillingly to school."*
As You Like It

Not a whole lot is known about Shakespeare's early life. The son of town baliff John Shakespeare and Mary Arden, he was born in 1564 (in Henley Street, 'The Birthplace') and baptised at Holy Trinity Church. In 1582 he married Anne Hathaway; he was eighteen, she was twenty-six. A daughter was born six months later and twins were born in 1585. Then, Shakespeare completely vanished (from the historical record, at least). All we have to explain his 'lost years' is legends like the Charlecote Park poaching tale (page 79). Shakespeare reappeared in 1592 as a London playwright, famous enough already to be attacked in print as an "upstart crow" (Robert Greene, *Groats-Worth of Wit*). His earliest published work was probably the poem *Venus and Adonis* (1593), although many of his plays pre-date this. By 1597 he was successful enough to buy Stratford's second-largest house for his family (New Place, costing £60) and in 1599 he became part-owner of London's new Globe Theatre. He retired to New Place in 1613 and died on his 52nd birthday in 1616, possibly after a local drinking spree (see page 113).

Stratford's transformation from obscure Midlands market town to international tourism hotspot started slowly and then snowballed. By 1759, New Place was attracting so many interested visitors that it was demolished out of spite by its owner, Francis Gastrell; he was driven out of town. Actor David Garrick held a 'Shakespeare Jubilee' at Stratford in 1769 and it was this which really kickstarted the growth in visitors (and in turn, increasing interest in Shakespeare by a more mainstream audience). The town capitalised upon this opportunity, preserving their older buildings and encouraging new constructions to adopt a 'Tudorbethan' style.

In 1844, showman P.T. Barnum's attempt to buy 'The Birthplace' house and ship it back to the United States spurred the formation of the Shakespeare Birthday Committee, which raised £3,000 to purchase the house (donors included Charles Dickens). This subsequently became the Shakespeare Birthplace Trust, which eventually acquired a raft of historic properties including Anne Hathaway's Cottage and New Place Gardens. Stratford's cult of Shakespeare ('Bardolatry') continued to grow, aided and abetted by the travel and tourism industry ...

"Stratford-on-Avon is universally regarded in the light of a Travel Shrine of world-wide interest and importance ... The homeland of Shakespeare has ever been, and always must be, regarded in the light of a place of pilgrimage."

Shakespeare-Land, The World's Great Travel Shrine, Great Western Railway 1924

Stratford now sees upwards of 2.5 million visitors annually, and is the destination most visited, beyond London, by overseas tourists. It doesn't take itself entirely seriously, thankfully; on his most recent visit the author was able to buy a first edition copy of *William Shakespeare's Star Wars*.

 *The Birthplace.*

Weir Brake Lock Weir.

Bidford Bridge.

Section 5

Stratford-upon-Avon to Bidford-on-Avon

Distance 15km
Start △ Recreation Ground, Stratford-upon-Avon SP 204 546/ CV37 7PY
Finish ◯ Bidford Bridge SP 099 517 / B50 4AD

Introduction

"It is Shakespeare's country, and these are the woods and fields where, as a boy, he roved and bird's-nested, and Avon and her tributaries the waters in which he fished and learned to swim."

Canoeing, William Bliss, 1934

This is a lovely adventure! The Avon wrenches free from Stratford-upon-Avon's gravitational pull and proceeds quietly through low-lying countryside peppered with chocolate-box villages, punctuated by frequent weirs to portage or paddle.

Launch points

Stratford-upon-Avon (Recreation Ground) SP 204 546 / CV37 7PY – Recreation Ground car park on river left, across the river from the Royal Shakespeare Theatre, 300m past Clopton Bridge. Expensive.

Binton Bridges SP 144 530 / CV37 8PW – the Four Alls Pub and Restaurant, river left above the bridges. Landing stage for patrons only.

Bidford Bridge SP 099 517 / B50 4AD – the Big Meadow, a large riverside car park on river left below the bridge. Note that you will be

automatically charged on entering. There is also a free 24-hour car park across the bridge, 100m from the water.

Description

To briefly summarise Section 4; you launch opposite the Royal Shakespeare Theatre, portage Stratford Trinity Lock, paddle past Lucy's Mill Weirs and pass beneath the A4390 bridge, leaving town.

The river drifts between overgrown banks alongside Sausage Island, named for its narrow 110m length. At the end of the island is the entrance to Shakespeare Marina, which is otherwise hidden by the river left bank. This development has been planned since the 1970s but was finally under construction in 2022.

Only a third of a kilometre below the bridges, the island presaging **Weir Brake Lock** is reached. Following the main channel ahead will bring you to the rocky weir. There is no barrier above and inspection will reveal that it is a fairly simple shoot (assuming sufficient water), dropping less than a metre. Note however that lurking at the base are boulders big enough, for completely hypothetical example, to take a notable chunk out of your completely brand-new canoe.

"The next object of interest is the small coppice known as the Wyre Brake, and here the bottom of the boat strikes with some force the stones of a broken-down wyre."

John Henry Garrett, *The Idyllic Avon*, 1906

Weir Brake Lock itself is located a little further downstream, accessed by the river left channel. It also goes by the name of Gordon Gray Lock, and it has previously been called Anonymous Lock; the Avon locks regularly

The GWR Bridge below Stratford-upon-Avon.

have multiple names, honouring donors and patrons who have supported the work of restoring the river. Weir Brake was built over 38 days in 1973 by boys from H.M. Borstal Hewell Grange (borstals were prisons for young offenders). It was the last on the river to be completed and a monument at the lock thanks those, *"without whose munificence the work could not have been completed or still less accomplished"*.

As Garrett indicated, the wooded hillside on river left is called Weir Brake, the name predating the current lock; this was the site of Stratford Watergate, removed in the 1820s. Watergates, also known as 'flash locks', were barriers which held back the water long enough for craft to pass over shallows, before releasing it dramatically.

A kilometre downstream, the rusty girders of the GWR Bridge used to carry the Stratford to Cheltenham line. The Great Western Railway's promotional bumf promised to deliver tourists to Stratford, *"on the banks of the Warwickshire Avon, one of the most picturesque streams in England"* (*Shakespeare-Land, The World's Great Travel Shrine*, 1924). You will spot cyclists whizzing past overhead, as the line is now the Stratford Greenway, a popular eight-kilometre cycle route. Not far after, the River Stour joins from river left. Like all of the Avon's tributaries, this reed-strewn Cotswold stream is easily missed.

Houses uphill on river right and the spire of All Saints Church seen ahead herald arrival at Luddington. Tradition has it that Shakespeare and Anne Hathaway were married in

Luddington Lock.

this church, in 1582. It is known that she was pregnant and that scandal was avoided by marrying outside Stratford, however the parish records were lost in a nineteenth-century fire, so there is no certainty that Luddington was the place. Just past the church, Luddington Weir lurks around a left bend, obscured by reed-strewn islands, with **Luddington Lock** adjacent on river right.

"The dam is rather high; the water pours over it from above down two or three small, steep weirs, which lie between as many in-and-out gravelly strands."

John Henry Garrett, *The Idyllic Avon* 1906
The author used to enjoy thrashing a white-water racing kayak down the weir during the annual Avon Descent Race, however it has been revamped with an uninviting covering of jumbled boulders and is now a likely portage.

Land to portage on either bank of the lock, which is directly alongside the weir. The left-hand bank is probably easiest, but portaging is made awkward by narrow steps and high landing stages at the downstream end. The village is a short walk away, however a sign at the lock warns, *'Sorry, no pubs, no shops'*.

Men from Gloucester Gaol built Luddington Lock (AKA Stan Clover Lock) in 1971. There were previously two locks; Upper Luddington Lock was circular, and traces of it survive in the basin, stonework and a depression in the ground to river right of the present lock. The ruins of Lower Luddington Lock are a short distance downstream, hidden in a reed-choked channel to the left of an island.

The village of Weston-on-Avon is a kilometre further on river left, pinpointed by the squat tower of fifteenth-century All Saints Church. The *Domesday Book* of 1086 recorded the village as having, *"six villans, four slaves and five female slaves and a mill"*, and it's not much bigger nowadays. The river now describes a three-kilometre loop around the village of Welford-on-Avon, reaching Binton Bridges at its northernmost bend. This tree-lined reach is among the most attractive on the whole river. The Avon is (unsurprisingly) bridged at Binton Bridges, widening around two islands with six stone arches on either side of the central, willow-draped island. A narrow packhorse bridge from 1216 only crossed half of the river, the rest had to be forded! It was replaced in 1793 by the current bridge, funded by popular subscription.

The Four Alls pub is on river left, upstream of the bridge. The pub's name is explained by a Victorian sign: *'A king who rules over all; a parson who prays for all; a soldier who fights for all; a farmer who pays for all'*. The pub is a pleasant place to land and dine, before heading on downstream to **Welford Lock**.

"Here, by the river, is an old mill, with some old houses by it, and some old trees, a weir with a rush of white foaming water; and to contrast and complete it all, the bend in the river makes a bay, in which the whole is as in a black glass mirrored. A place Gainsborough might have painted."

James Thorne,
Rambles by Rivers: The Avon 1845

Upper Welford Lock is now buried on the wooded and overgrown island between the modern Welford Lock and weir, but Thorne's

📷 Binton Bridges.

description still holds up. Even before you factor in its location beside one of the most attractive villages in the country, this is a gorgeous spot. Welford Lock (AKA W. A. Cadbury Lock, built 1971, again by Gloucester prisoners) occupies the river right channel. Portage along the meadow on river right.

The weir is a shallow-angled slope curving along the course of the river, easily approached by paddling around the river left end of the floating barrier. It flows into a shallow rapid around an island, which may need wading in summer. To river left of the weir is the converted former mill; when this closed in 1958, there had been a working mill here since at least 1291.

The Avon flows south from Welford Lock before bending west at the foot of Cress Hill. If you manage to land on the river left footpath, it's possible to climb up through woods and meadows to a viewpoint and picnic area.

"One of the prettiest views to be anywhere obtained on the River Avon ... it needs to be seen itself, and it is too wide and panoramic for representation in a picture."

John Henry Garrett, *The Idyllic Avon* 1906

It's also easier from shore to spot the remains of Lower Welford Lock, built in 1827 and *"quite a picturesque ruin"* according to Garrett. Two parallel lines of stones survive at the water's edge, discernible even on the OS map. The weir was dredged out in the 1970s.

The remaining four kilometres heading west to Bidford-on-Avon maintain the pleasant scenery and quiet surrounds. Hillborough Manor (where Charles II reputedly hid his treasure after the Battle of Worcester in

Welford Weir.

Bidford Grange Lock.

1651, and also apparently haunted) is passed, barely noticeably, on river right. Shortly after, **Bidford Grange Lock** (AKA Pilgrim Lock) can be portaged along the river left bank (beside Pilgrim Lock campsite), otherwise the small rocky weir on the river right side of the island is a fairly simple descent. The lock took Gloucester gaol's inmates six hard weeks to construct in 1970, hampered by winter floods and collapsing banks. Directly downstream, the Avon speeds along a narrow channel passing a lengthy wooded island.

"One of those green, reed, rush and osier–grown islands … the cool haunt of small birds and aquatic animals."

John Henry Garrett, *The Idyllic Avon* 1906

If you explore the overgrown channel to river right of the island, you'll find yourself in view of Bidford Grange Country Club's golfers. This was the site of Grange Lock, with two mills producing corn and paper. OS maps still located the weir and lock here into the previous decade. Only a few stones from the weir survive among the reeds.

Another wooded island and also a couple of marina entrances are passed approaching Barton, where the final lock of the day is encountered. **Barton Lock** (AKA Elsie and Hiram Billington Lock) was built by inmates of Redditch Borstal, originally utilising gates salvaged from a Thames lock. Portaging is easiest along the river right bank. The small weir on the river left channel is rock-strewn, but it's not hard to discern a clear channel to paddle through. Two campsites (including the Cottage of Content pub), are a short distance

Barton Weir.

away from the weir, along a footpath. On our most recent visit, the beach on the island below the weir was strewn with otter spraint. The Church of St Lawrence's square tower looms over your arrival at Bidford-on-Avon. Bidford Bridge, with its eight arches, was constructed in 1482 by monks from Alcester Priory. After Charles I's army demolished it to cover their retreat in 1644, stones from the same (now-dissolved) priory were used to repair it. It has seen many more repairs, including in 2015 when a tractor near-destroyed it.

"Bidford Bridge is one of the old style, with low arches of varying size and shape, the passage way over it being narrow as it was the original Roman road, known as Icknield Street or, locally, as Buckle Street, which crossed the river here."

John Henry Garrett, *The Idyllic Avon* 1906

The Roman road actually crossed via a ford 100m upstream from the bridge; dredging revealed a causeway supported by bronze- and iron-tipped oak piles, driven into the riverbed by army engineers. In Early Medieval times this became known as Byda's Ford, giving the village its name.

The Big Meadow car park is on river left below the bridge; in summer this will be a busy spot, with other paddlers and the general public splashing about.

Boat Lane, Welford-on-Avon.

Welford-on-Avon

Welford is well worth a wander. Annoyingly, it can't be accessed directly from Welford Lock and instead it's a one-kilometre walk from the Four Alls pub at Binton Bridges. The half-timbered thatched cottages leading towards the Avon on Boat Lane are the literal definition of chocolate-box scenery; Ten-Penny Cottage has actually appeared on Cadbury's chocolate boxes. Close by, the Church of St Peter dates from the twelfth century and was restored by George Gilbert Scott in 1867. Further along Church Lane, the Bell Inn claims to be the pub where Shakespeare drank before catching a (fatal) fever on the way home (see page 113). South along High Street is Welford's remarkable weathervane-topped maypole. This has stood on the village green, proudly priapic, since at least the sixteenth century. It made Robert Aickman (founder of the Inland Waterways Association, fantasy fiction author and occultist*) feel all pagan: *"A sturdy symbol, seventy feet high and painted like a barber's trade mark, emblem and relic of that Old Religion which the Christians so cruelly persecuted"* (*Portraits of Rivers*, 1953).

*Read his biography on Wikipedia, it's an absolute treat.

Harvington Weir.

Below Cleeve Hill.

Section 6

Bidford-on-Avon to Evesham

Distance 13.1km
Start △ Bidford Bridge SP 099 517 / B50 4AD
Finish ○ Abbey Bridge, Evesham SP 033 431 / WR11 4BY

Introduction

"The garden of England ... In the spring the miles and miles of blossom are a sight to be remembered, while the air is scented beyond the power of the pen to describe."

Alec R. Ellis, *The Book of Canoeing*, 1935

Welcome to the Vale of Evesham! The Avon flows right through the heart of this fertile region of fruit farms, orchards and market gardens, steering a course to the historic town of Evesham.

Launch points

Bidford Bridge SP 099 517 / B50 4AD – the Big Meadow, a large riverside car park on river left below the bridge. Note that you will be automatically charged on entering. There is also a free 24-hour car park across the bridge, 100m from the water.

Marlcliff SP 093 505 / B50 4NT – small riverside parking area on river left at the end of a rough track leading downhill from The Bank in Marlcliff.

Cleeve Prior SP 080 499 / WR11 8JZ – footpath on river left leading a short distance, under a height barrier, to a small parking area at the end of Mill Lane. Road is steep and in poor condition.

Offenham Weir SP 065 470 / WR11 8QT – river left, launch at the ford track leading directly

105

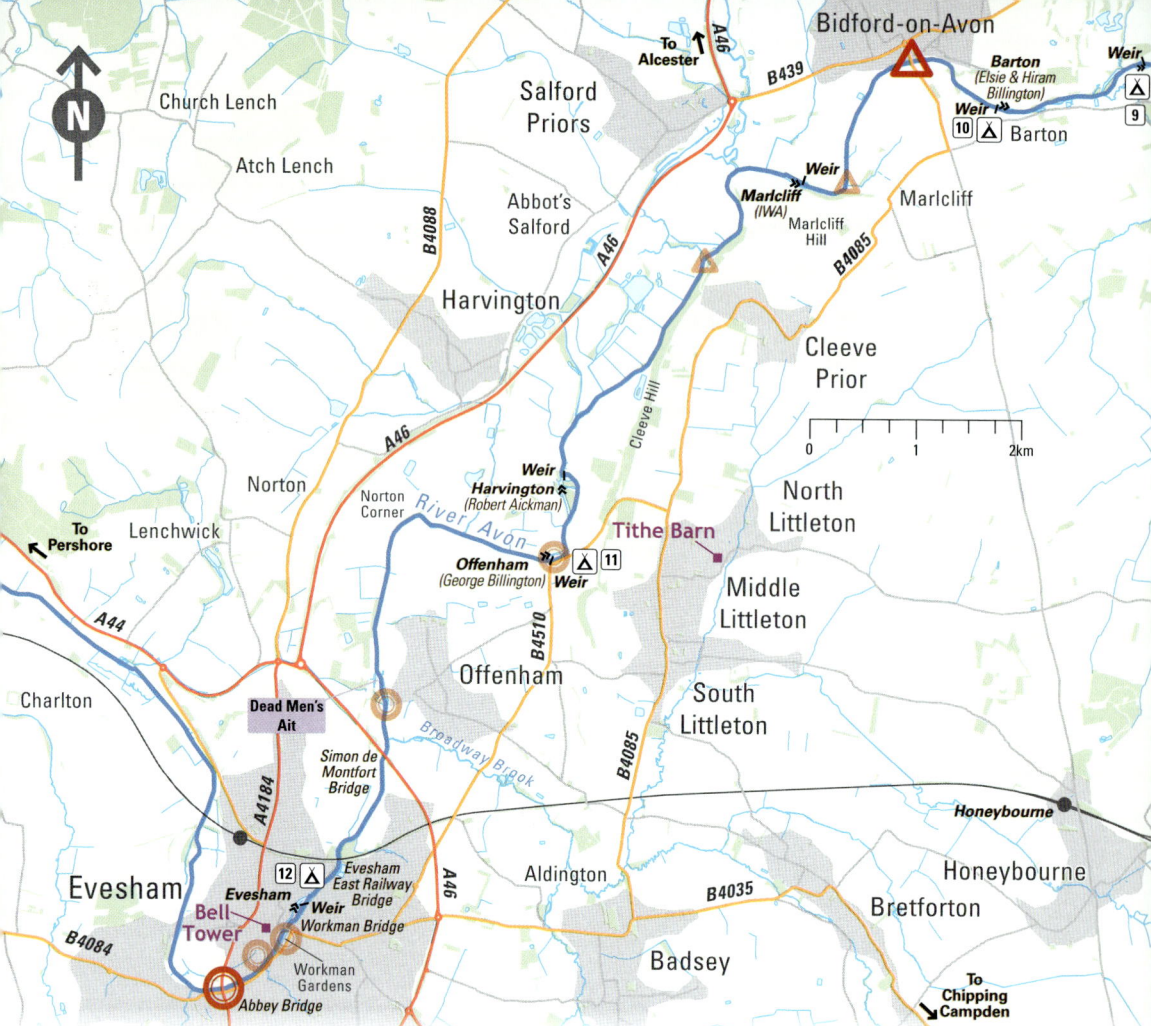

to the weir. A tiny layby on a bend in front of houses. Parking also available at the Fish and Anchor Inn, with their permission.

Offenham SP 049 457 / WR11 8RS – small parking area and picnic space beside the ferry slipway on river left at the end of Boat Lane, alongside the Bridge Inn.

Evesham (Waterside Gardens) SP 038 434 / WR11 1BU – roadside parking on river left along Waterside Road.

Evesham (Crown Meadow) SP 035 432 / WR11 4SS – pay and display car parks on river right across Crown Meadow from the river, open in summer only.

Evesham (Abbey Bridge) SP 033 431 / WR11 4BY – Viaduct Meadow car park, on river right directly below Abbey Bridge. Pay and display.

Description

The crowds enjoying the river around Bidford Bridge are nothing new; from the Victorian era until the Second World War, this attractive village with its Georgian High Street was a popular daytrip from Birmingham. Novelist

📷 *Marlcliff.*

Barbara Comyns wrote a semi-autobiographical novel about her upbringing in Bidford;

"Awful people called trippers used to come to our village on Public Holidays ... They hired boats from Hollands and on the river they went, but often ended in it. They couldn't row or punt, but splashed, screamed, showed their braces and got drunk ... they really were beastly and were always giving the village girls babies and making an awful noise, the babies as well as the trippers."

Barbara Comyns, *Sisters by a River* 1947

The site of a former watergate is marked by shallow islands downstream of the bridge. The flow was controlled by adjustable paddles and rymers until the watergate was removed in the 1950s.

The Avon bends south upon leaving Bidford and maintains this course for just a kilometre until Marlcliff Corner, where Marlcliff Hill rudely forces it west. This 30m-high cliff of marl (clay) is densely tree-covered, with dog roses adding colour.

"A bare scar of green and red marl, here covered with long gray grass and dotted with old thorn and crab trees, here clothed with hanging woods of maple, ash, and other trees, straggled over and smothered with ivy, wild rose, and clematis."

Arthur Quiller-Couch,
The Warwickshire Avon 1892

Marlcliff Lock (AKA Inland Waterways Association Lock) is possibly the wildest on the river, tucked beneath the river left scarp with no road access. Due to the marl clay's hardness, the Gloucester prisoners struggled with construction in 1969 and the lock channel had to be blasted out by Royal Engineers.

Paddle around the barrier above the weir to inspect. The weir is a messy (and slightly

Marlcliff Weir.

overgrown) slope of boulders, down which a route can be picked, with care. Below, the water flows quickly among reedy channels. If portaging around the lock, either launch below this or cross the island to launch below the weir.

The following kilometres enter the Vale of Evesham proper.

"... a vast green plain, soft and warmly sunlit, dotted with villages that clustered around square stone towers, flecked with the lighter green where the willows traced the meanderings of the Avon."

Harry Hopkins, *England is Rich* 1957

Although this idyllic description still holds true, modern industrial farming dominates the landscape beyond the river; stepping ashore or driving shuttle, you soon encounter enormous glasshouses, vast fields of covered fruit and seemingly limitless orchards.

The River Arrow, a sizeable tributary winding south from Redditch, joins the Avon on river right at a left bend. Garrett explored upstream on the Arrow; *"... into this mouth you may pull your boat, and ascending the tortuous tributary for some hundreds of yards, find shady spots in which to lie concealed from the observation of trippers on the Avon"* (*The Idyllic Avon*, 1906).

After another kilometre, the steep wooded river left bank is resumed when the Avon comes alongside Cleeve Hill. This was the site of Cleeve Lock, the star attraction for daytrippers on boat tours from Bidford; Garrett called it, *"perhaps, the finest place for boating on the Avon"* (*The Idyllic Avon*, 1906).

A ruined stone wall juts out on river right at SP 080 499, marking the site of Cleeve Lock. It's worth landing to explore the overgrown lock chamber, a well-preserved diamond shape, left high and dry by dredging. Cleeve Weir was breached in 1939 and Cleeve Mill was demolished during the 1960's 'restoration'. A ford ran below, used in 1265 by Prince Edward to cut off Simon de Montfort before the Battle of Evesham. Bodies found buried alongside the ford in 1824 were assumed to be drowned soldiers of Montford's. They were re-buried at the Owen Stone (see page 110).

On river left, a steep rough road leads up to Cleeve Prior, a village of honey-coloured Cotswold limestone cottages with a sixteenth-century manor house. If you find yourself at fifteenth-century St Andrew's Church, seek out the grave of Sara Charlett who died in 1693, aged 309!

Cleeve Lock's lost heritage is thankfully recalled by the delightful **Harvington Lock**, two kilometres downstream. The weir is encountered first, a long and gently sloping structure dropping off to river left beneath a walkway. Hold off from paddling this until you've explored the lock area. The river channel splits. The left

◎ *Harvington Weir.*

(centre) channel leads to a covered dry dock. This is the original Robert Aickman Lock, built by the Upper Avon Navigation Trust (1969), on the site of the original circular lock. The far river right channel leads to Robert Aickman New Lock, built in 1982 after the first one kept silting up. On river left directly below the New Lock is Harvington Mill, a substantial ruin almost completely obscured by ivy and other greenery.

Portage New Lock on river right, otherwise head back up and paddle the weir. The weir feeds into a riffly channel, only re-joining the navigation channel after 500m. This whole lovely locale is dedicated to Aickman's memory, and there is a memorial to him alongside New Lock. He founded the Inland Waterways Association in 1946 and fought hard for the Avon to be restored as a navigation: *"Below Stratford all is ruin on the river for many miles"* (*Portraits of Rivers*, 1953).

Just 300m after the channels reconverge, a sharp right bend signifies the approach of **Offenham Lock**. The blind bend, an ominous-looking barrier and stern warning signs are somewhat off-putting ... however, if you *"Stiffen the sinews, summon up the blood"* (*Henry V*) and venture past the barrier into the river left channel, you'll find yourself faced

◎ *Offenham Lock.*

by the smallest weir on the Navigation, with tourists wading across it! Overlooked by the Fish and Anchor Inn (a campsite), Offenham Weir is a driveable ford, marked on maps as a footpath. Size isn't everything, however; the smooth lip can of course generate a powerful stopper in higher flows. Below the weir, the river ripples across rapids channelled by waving water-crowfoot, with low branches to duck.

Offenham Lock (AKA George Billington Lock, named for a donor who died a week after completion in 1969) is most memorable for the quirky lock keeper's hut, a cylindrical tower built in 1981 and resembling a miniature lighthouse. It was designed to be flood-proof, but has been out of commission since 2007, when ... you guessed it, it was flooded out. Portaging, it is easiest to re-enter the water on the river left side of the lock.

The Fish and Anchor Inn is an obvious place to head for some shore leave (under new management, thankfully, after featuring in a 2007 episode of TV show *Ramsey's Kitchen Nightmares*). Footpaths lead from the pub steeply uphill to the Owen Stone (the remains of a medieval cross, perched atop a prehistoric mound) and the villages of South Littleton and Middle Littleton, the latter boasting a huge tithe barn dating from 1367–77 and now in the National Trust's care.

About 300m below Offenham Lock, the remains of Lower Harvington Lock are well hidden on river left. Depending on the water level (and reed density) it is sometimes possible to float among the gate supports and walls, surviving from 1820.

Bredon Hill will be first spotted at some point along this stretch, rising behind Evesham.

📷 *Offenham Weir and the Fish and Anchor.*

Offenham.

The sharp left bend directing the Avon south towards Evesham is called Norton Corner. The river right embankment was the course of the Redditch and Evesham Railway, now a footpath. Behind, the slopes are covered with apple trees. Cue William Bliss ... *"The glory of Evesham is, of course, its orchards, and the best time to come down the Avon is a late Easter or an early Whitsuntide ..."* (*The Heart of England by Waterway*, 1933).

The large island 1.5 kilometres below Norton Corner is Dead Men's Ait (*Ait*, Old English for 'island'). The name references human remains discovered in the eighteenth century, believed to be Welsh soldiers massacred in the aftermath of the Battle of Evesham. The downstream end of the island is marked by the Bridge Inn on river left. This spot was an important crossing point; the Old London Road negotiated, *"a narrow stone bridge for footmen"* (John Leland, *The Itinerary*, 1535–43) and when this collapsed, a ferry service operated, continuing until recent years.

Offenham is a short walk up the road from the pub. The village, now surrounded by glasshouses, takes its name from King Offa of Mercia (the Dyke builder) who resided here. A left turn up Main Street will take you past the Church of St Mary and St Milburga (restored in 1862, named after a saintly noblewoman possessing power over birds) to the village's centrepiece.

"... standing up in the centre of the street – a tall gailey painted May-pole, telling of the days when it was "impossible to sleep on a May-day morning"
James Thorne,
Rambles by Rivers: The Avon 1845

Maypole dancing still takes place here in early June, during Offenham's Wake Week.

The boundary of Evesham is marked by the concrete Simon de Montford Bridge carrying

Evesham Weir.

the A46 Evesham bypass. After Evesham East Railway Bridge a kilometre further, Evesham Marina is on river left, followed by the slipway of Gas Works Wharf on river right (no gasworks since the 80s); this is noteworthy as it gives access to Evesham Caravan Site, a possible camping spot.

Evesham Weir is a massive construction spanning diagonally across the river and marked out by a floating barrier and raised walkway. Although **Evesham Lock** is located 150m further downstream on river right (beside the distinctive A-frame lock house, built in 1976 over a sluice and mill stream), there is a signposted portage path close to hand on river left, albeit close to the weir's 'event horizon'. This leads alongside the weir face into the weir pool. The weir lands on rocks, making it uninviting if not exactly unpaddleable:

"These violent delights have violent ends" (*Romeo and Juliet*). Don't paddle the tempting-looking chute, the former 'punt rollers' are gone, leaving exposed metal bolts.

Workman Bridge was historically the end of the Upper, and start of the Lower, Avon Navigations. The bridge was built in 1856, named after Mayor Henry Workman. The previous medieval bridge was heavily damaged during the Civil War. Below the bridge, trees and public parks line both banks.

Workman Gardens line the river left bank; these were created in 1864 on the former site of warehouses, using foundations recycled from the old bridge. The whalebone arch was erected in 1906; the bones (three centuries old) were replaced by replicas in 2012. Evesham's River Festival is based here for several days every July.

Bidford-on-Avon and Shakespeare

"Bidford, where is alleged to have occurred the drinking bout which lead to Shakespeare's death." Robert Aickman in *Portraits of Rivers* 1953

Bidford-on-Avon's claim to fame is that Shakespeare possibly drank himself to death there. Nothing concrete is known about what ended the playwright's life. Half a century after his death, Vicar of Stratford-upon-Avon John Ward reported tavern gossip that, *"Shakespeare, Drayton, and Ben Jonson had a merry meeting and, it seems, drank too hard, for Shakespeare died of a fever there contracted"*. Bidford's Falcon Inn enterprisingly claimed that theirs was the offending pub and that Shakespeare had been a regular, showing off his supposed chair and tankard. A 1762 magazine article embellished this with a tale of Shakespeare and friends joining a drinking contest against the 'Bidford Topers', where the writers became 'intolerably intoxicated' and slept under a crab apple tree. The tree became known as Shakespeare's crab, which survived until being stripped apart by nineteenth-century souvenir hunters (Crabtree Farm on the B439 marks the spot). The Falcon Inn was on High Street and is now a private home.

Abbey Gardens are on river right, overlooked by the imposing 33-metre Bell Tower, the only remnant of Evesham Abbey. The Abbey was founded in 702 AD on the site where Eove, the shepherd who gave the town its name, saw a vision of the Virgin Mary. It saw various collapses and rebuilds until the Bell Tower was completed in 1539, squeezed alongside the spire and tower respectively of All Saints and St Lawrence's parish churches. Only a year after the tower was completed, Henry VIII's commissioners came along to dissolve the abbey and the townsfolk raised £100 to keep the tower. A stone memorial in front of it marks the original burial place of Simon de Montfort. Abbey Bridge is fairly new (2014), replacing a 1928 concrete structure. Viaduct Meadow car park is on river right, directly after it.

Workman Bridge, Evesham.

📷 *Leaving Evesham.*

Cropthorne Mill and Fladbury Weir.

Section 7

Evesham to Pershore

Distance 16.5km
Start △ Abbey Bridge, Evesham SP 033 431 / WR11 4BY
Finish ○ Recreation Ground, Pershore SO 952 460 / WR10 1EY

Introduction

"Shooting down the weir and with great stir below upon gravelly reaches about Chadbury Mill, gliding peacefully under the woods and lawns of Fladbury to another weir and another mill, it winds along to Pershore."

Arthur Granville Bradley,
The Rivers and Streams of England 1909

This long paddle between abbey towns is broken up by just three locks and weirs. Two of these are exceptionally beautiful and either would justify the outing alone.

Launch points

Evesham (Abbey Bridge) SP 033 431 / WR11 4BY – Viaduct Meadow car park, on river right directly below Abbey Bridge. Pay and display.

Evesham (Hampton Ferry) SP 029 436 / WR11 4AF – car park on river right at end of Boat Lane. Slipway at end of lane. Launching fee charged.

Fladbury (Fladbury Mill Meadow) SO 996 459 / WR10 2QA – roadside parking area, directly south of the village on river right. Cross the road and follow one of the permissive paths across Fladbury Mill Meadow to access the river, below Fladbury Lock. Or, walk 100m into the village and launch from the small public park, upstream of the weir.

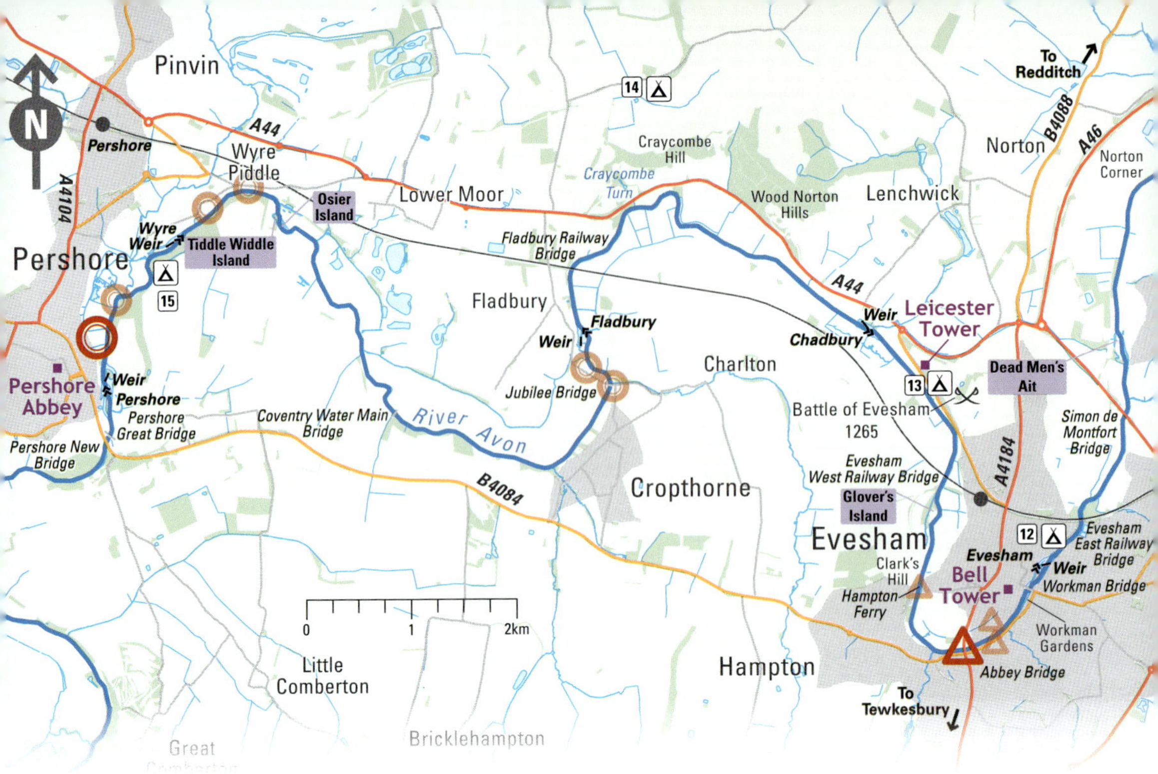

Fladbury (Jubilee Bridge) SP 000 456 / WR10 3NG – Jubilee Bridge Picnic Place, on river left above the bridge. Car park with a height barrier.

Wyre Piddle (beside Anchor Inn) SO 965 474 / WR10 2JB – a public footpath leads 20m from Main Road to the river (river right), through the gate signed *'Parking & Gardens for Patrons only'*. However, it is overgrown and inaccessible at present (2022). This may change / needs to change.

Wyre Piddle (Smith's Meadow) SO 961 473 / WR10 2JD – public recreation space on river right. Limited roadside parking on Church Street, outside the church. Enter the meadow and carry 100m down to the water.

Pershore (Avon Meadows Community Wetland) SO 951 461 / WR10 1EY – recreation area on river right with parking leading down to the riverside, accessed from King George's Way, beside the entrance to the football ground. Local authorities intermittently open and close the site.

Pershore (Recreation Ground) SO 952 460 / WR10 1EY – public park on river right. Pay and display car park on King George's Way, 150m across park. Alternatively, park roadside on Cherry Orchard.

Wyre Piddle.

Evesham.

Description

Evesham's centre is enclosed within a tight loop of the river. It is a surprise then, paddling the second half of the loop which bends north, how quickly the town falls back from the banks and is largely unobtrusive or hidden by greenery. The confluence of the River Isbourne is passed on river left just after Abbey Bridge, followed by St Andrew's Church with its tall Perpendicular-style tower topped by four pinnacles. There are pleasant views of the abbey Bell Tower (and the two parish churches alongside it), back across Corporation Meadow ... and that is all you really see of Evesham. The wires strung across the river at Hampton Ferry mark your exit from town. The ferry originated to serve the Abbey and was revived by the Huxley family, who have run the camping site and later caravan park on river right, for approaching a century. They opened Raphael's Restaurant beside the ferry in 1978 and it is something of a local institution, serving, *'High quality food in generous portions for a reasonable price'.*

The orchards of Clark's Hill, formerly the Abbey's vineyard, line the river left banks for the kilometre to Evesham West Railway Bridge. Glover's Island is also passed on river left, barely being an island beyond having a muddy back channel. Frank Glover was a volatile nineteenth-century local who would challenge all who displeased him to bare-knuckle fights on the island.

The river bends north-west and draws close to the road, which remains nearby on river right for the following four kilometres, unseen but often heard. In 1265, the Battle of Evesham

◎ *Chadbury Weir.*

played out on the hillside behind. The supposed site where Earl of Leicester Simon de Montfort met his death is marked by an obelisk, erected in 1845 in the grounds of nineteenth-century Abbey Manor. The obelisk is obscured by trees but the Gothic-style Abbey Manor is glimpsed once or twice, for example behind the inlet of Sankey Marine (a ramshackle redbrick marina, with camping possible). About 200m further downstream, the Leicester Tower (1842) is a battlemented redbrick octagonal folly, honouring Montfort himself;

"THE FATHER AND FOUNDER OF THE BRITISH HOUSE OF COMMONS"

The folly can be visited and is only 100m from the river, however the permissive path around the battlefield approaches from the lane behind, so this is best saved for an excursion while driving shuttle.

The Leicester Tower can also be spotted looking back upstream from **Chadbury Lock**. The 'Picturesque Movement' of the eighteenth century consisted of slightly pompous men visiting beauty spots not to enjoy them, but to judge whether they fitted arbitrary rules of picturesque beauty when viewed through a small mirror, with their backs turned. Chadbury Lock seems to have ticked all their boxes;

◎ *Leicester Tower.*

"So rich a landscape that nature seems not to require the assistance of art, in the language of modern refinement, either to correct her coarse expression by removing a hill or docking a tree, or to supply her careless and tasteless omissions for the purpose of rendering her more completely picturesque."

Picturesque Views on the Upper, or Warwickshire Avon, Samuel Ireland, 1795

Ireland did have a point, Chadbury is a lovely spot. The lock lies along the river left bank. It was rebuilt 1952–3 by Royal Engineers, drafted in to save Evesham from losing its waterfront; this was the Army's first civilian project. Like many of the locks downstream of Evesham (the old 'Lower' Avon) it is preserved close to its original state, with brick and stone sides (as opposed to steel) and wooden gates. Get out to explore on river left, but it isn't necessary to portage around the lock.

Paddle around to the river right side of the lock island and past the floating barrier to reach the very convenient portage steps along the river left edge of Chadbury Weir. The weir face itself is gently sloping, wide and shallow. At summer levels it is so benign that the author, stuck here for one long, hot day providing safety cover for a kayak race, once *dozed off* while side-surfing the stopper at the base. Paddling it is a pleasure, although all the obvious disclaimers apply. The weir saw restoration work in the 1990s, with eel and elver passes added, and the mill building on river right has been converted to a house; but it is hard to believe that Ireland wouldn't recognise this spot. He might however have been surprised by the sight of Jeremy Clarkson descending the weir in a Ford Transit hovercraft, in a stunt for the *Top Gear* TV show!

Below Chadbury Lock.

The Wood Norton hills rise 100m above the Avon on river right; leaf cover allowing, you may spot Wood Norton Hall on the hillside. Currently the BBC's Technical and Operational Training Centre, during the Second World War it listened in on foreign broadcasts and was the BBC's designated broadcasting centre in the event of invasion. A vast nuclear bunker was constructed post-war, from which the BBC would have broadcast cheery 'Keep calm and carry on' messages following a nuclear attack. Earlier in the twentieth century, Wood Norton was a royal residence! Both the Duc d'Orleans (a pretender to French throne) and King Manuel of Portugal (deposed in 1910) were housed here in exile.

With the long profile of Bredon Hill becoming increasing prominent beyond the river left bank *"When Bredon Hill puts on his hat, Ye men of the Vale, beware of that"*: (traditional weather rhyme), the boat moorings of Craycombe Turn are reached. Above this point where the Avon bends south towards Fladbury, eighteenth-century Craycombe House is perched. While not visible from the water, it's worthy of note; it was bought in the 1890s by George Perrott, nephew of the George Perrott who repaired the river in the 1760s, and in the 1930s it was the home of novelist Francis Brett Young. Brett Young was a sort of Midlands Thomas Hardy, his 'Mercian novels' set in a fictionalised representation of the region.

Fladbury Paddle Club is located on river right, directly below Fladbury Railway Bridge. Founded in 1972, the club has achieved outstanding success in marathon and sprint

 *Fladbury Paddle Club.*

Fladbury Weir.

racing, and has produced numerous national and Olympic athletes, from a village population of 750. Fladbury (Old English *Fledanburg*: 'floodland-fortified town'), an attractive village with many half-timbered houses, was home to William Sandys ('Waterworks Sandys') who in 1636 commenced the work of making the Avon navigable. The pinnacled Church of St John the Baptist was restored in 1871 but originates from the twelfth century, on monastic land granted by Ethelred of Mercia in 691AD. However, the scenic highlights of the village (and possibly the whole lower river) are found around **Fladbury Lock**.

John Henry Garrett summed up the spot succinctly: *"A fine weir slants down from near one mill towards the other"* (*The Idyllic Avon*, 1906). Fladbury Lock sits along the river left bank. The island to the right of this is occupied by Cropthorne Mill, a towering redbrick monolith. The mill abuts directly onto the weir; this is a large sloping drop with the main flow concentrated alongside Cropthorne Mill and a further expanse of (normally) dry weir face stretching downstream to Fladbury Mill on the river right bank. Both mills have survived all floods in their present forms since the eighteenth century and were in operation until the 1930s. They are now private residences. Fladbury Mill *"with its curious jumble of timbers, machinery, floors at all levels and angles ... a perfect storehouse of subjects for the artist"* (Charles Showell, *Shakespeare's Avon, from source to Severn*, 1901) served Fladbury by powering some of the first electric street lamps in the UK. Wild swimming pioneer

Cropthorne.

Roger Deakin described swimming here (including jumping out of the window of Cropthorne Mill!) in his influential book *Waterlog*. So, it is all rather pleasant! The lock is easily portaged along the river left bank. Alternatively, consider paddling past the floating barrier and weir and portaging down the dry part of the weir face (the author remembers a K1 marathon race where you had to jostle with other competitors to portage *up* it, in his case leading to an embarrassing swim). Another option is lining your boat down the dedicated channel at the weir's edge, but this can be slippery. Paddling the weir is tremendous fun in low water, at other times, *"The better part of valour is discretion"* (*Henry IV*).

Merry Brook joins on river left, just above Jubilee Bridge (a concrete arch from 1933) with its picnic area. Just downstream was Cropthorne Watergate, a flash lock removed in 1961; brick and masonry remains are still visible. The village of Cropthorne is perched atop a slope on river left, with gardens reaching down to the water.

"An exceedingly pretty rural village. It is situated on high ground away from the main road, and overlooking the river ... The cottages are humble, timber-framed thatched dwellings, but quiet and pleasant looking."

James Thorne,
Rambles by Rivers: The Avon 1845

Yet another enclave of picturesque half-timbered houses, Cropthorne can be explored on foot from Jubilee Bridge. The twelfth century church of St Michael displays a beautiful carved stone cross head from 800 AD which was discovered in the eighteenth century,

📷 *Wyre Lock.*

described by Pevsner as, *"The best piece of Anglo-Saxon art in the county"*.

"The reaches below Cropthorne struck us as singularly beautiful. From a fringe of fantastic pollard willows, out of whose decayed trunks grew the wild rose and bramble, orchards and pastures swelled."

Arthur Quiller-Couch,
The Warwickshire Avon, 1892

This *"singularly beautiful"* 4.5 kilometres ambles north-west with the only landmarks being the bridge carrying the piped Coventry Water Main, and Osier Island to river right of the navigation channel, closely followed by Tiddle Widdle Island to river left. Osier Island ('*osier*' is an archaic word for willow trees) has a house accessible only by water, you will envy the owner.

The back gardens of Wyre Piddle now occupy the steep river right slope, including the terraced garden of the Anchor Inn, which has been serving river users since the sixteenth century. The name 'Wyre' has Celtic roots; ver / wær / wer are all variations on 'fishing station'; in other words, a weir. 'Piddle' you can work out for yourself, in this case it references a nearby stream which also gives its name to a local brewery.

The *wyre* / weir comes along soon enough; a marina is passed on river right and moored boats line the banks approaching **Wyre Lock**. The lock, on river left, is diamond-shaped. It's the only Avon lock of this shape today, previously they were all like this (or circular) to reduce erosion to the earthen walls when the paddles opened. The portage along the river left bank can be hard work; it's quite long and sometimes overgrown. The two successive weirs located to river right are sadly not cleanly paddleable, landing on rocks. Back on the water, Wyre Mill looms over a sluice on river right. This massive nineteenth century corn mill (*"the ugliest mill, of which the Avon is ashamed."*

📷 *Wyre Mill.*

Charles Showell, *Shakespeare's Avon, from source to Severn* 1901) was converted into a social club by the Lower Avon Navigation Trust and the site includes a maintenance wharf, leisure boat facilities and a campsite.

Pershore Lock is just 1.6km downstream, the closest gap between locks on the Avon. However, just before you reach it, the banks open on river right to reveal park benches with a football field behind; this is the Recreation Ground in Pershore, your destination.

"One of the few towns or villages that the river actually visits; these are usually found a little to the left, over the hill, or across the meadow, or behind the trees – never near, and seldom in sight."

Charles Showell, *Shakespeare's Avon, from source to Severn* 1901

Simon de Montfort

Simon de Montfort, Earl of Leicester, was a controversial and contradictory figure. Montford led the baronial opposition ('The Second Baron's War') to the increasingly tyrannical rule of Henry III, capturing the King and his son Edward at Lewes in 1264. Now de facto ruler of England, Montford set up the first elected parliament in England to include ordinary (i.e. non-noble) people. However, his radical reforming zeal seems to have unsettled even his supporters and he was possibly just too far ahead of his time. Edward escaped in 1265 and raised an army which ambushed Montford (by carrying the banners of Montford's son), trapping him in the loop of the Avon at Evesham. Chronicler Robert of Gloucester described the Battle of Evesham as, *"the murder of Evesham, for battle it was none"*.

Montford's heavily mutilated body was buried at Evesham Abbey. The grave became a popular shrine, so an irritated Henry III had the remains moved to a secret location. Montford has been lauded as a founder of representative democracy, but was also responsible for appalling expulsions and massacres of Jews. More can be learned about Montford and the Battle of Evesham at Evesham's Almonry Museum, housed in a fourteenth-century building near the Abbey Bell Tower.

Pershore

"Pleasant Pershore ... is just large enough to be a town ... where there is little to do, and yet you have never finished with it."

John Henry Garrett, *The Idyllic Avon* 1906

Pershore gets its name from the pears sold locally, or possibly from 'osier bank' (*osier*: a willow tree). This small town stretches parallel to the river along High Street and Bridge Street, a contender for the finest Georgian street in England.

Imposing Perrott House, at 17 Bridge Street, was built in 1760 for the Perrott family, who owned and restored the Navigation. The town's affluence didn't always extend to all; rural poverty led to unrest in the 1760s and 1830s.

"Several hundred persons, chiefly women and children, assembled in the neighbourhood of Pershore, in order to intercept and pillage some vessels, laden with corn and meal ..."

Birmingham Gazette 1767

Dragoons were sent to the town and the Riot Act read.

Pershore Abbey originated as a wooden building established by Oswald of Mercia in 689 and grew in its current stone form from 1100. The Abbey was demolished in 1540, during the dissolution of the monasteries. Pershore's populace coughed up £400, only sufficient to save its four-pinnacled tower and transepts (one of which collapsed in 1686, hence the church's peculiar proportions).

Pershore Abbey.

Above Great Comberton.

Beside the Recreation Ground in Pershore.

Section 8

Pershore to Eckington Bridge

Distance 11km
Start Recreation Ground, Pershore SO 952 460 / WR10 1EY
Finish Eckington Bridge SO 922 423 / WR10 3DD

Introduction

"Below Pershore the river so winds that whether you row down stream or up, Bredon Hill will be found the dominant feature in the landscape. But whether a passing cloud paints it purple, or the sun shines on it, lighting the grassy slopes, and showing every bush and quarry on the sides, it is always a beautiful background."

Arthur Quiller-Couch,
The Warwickshire Avon, 1892

Below Pershore, the market gardens of the Vale of Evesham are replaced by a mixed countryside of meadows, sheep and cows. The Avon winds back and forth amidst this pastoral idyll, always watched over by looming Bredon Hill. A mid-paddle shore trip to ascend the hill is a statutory requirement for all paddlers.

Launch points

Pershore (Recreation Ground) SO 952 460 / WR10 1EY – public park on river right. Pay and display car park on King George's Way, 150m across park. Alternatively, park roadside on Cherry Orchard.

Pershore (New Bridge) SO 952 450 / WR10 3NW – car park on river left between the old and new Pershore bridges. Height barrier.

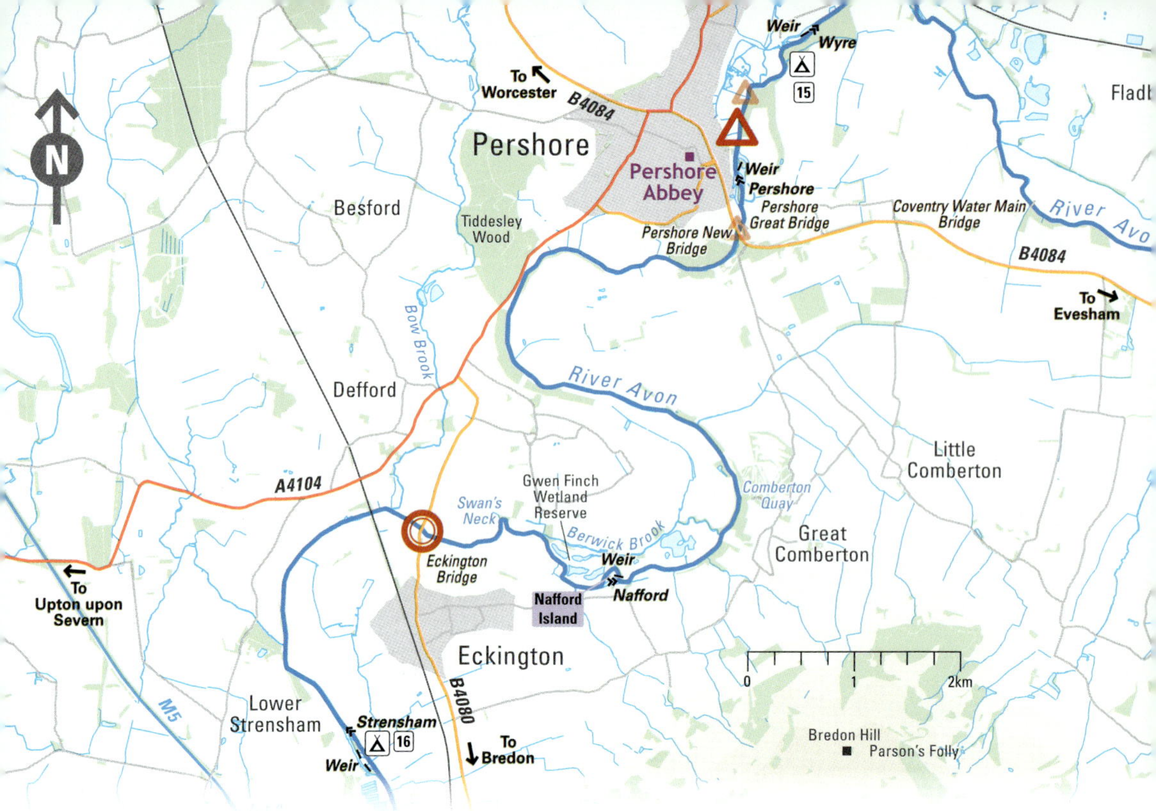

Eckington Bridge SO 922 423 / WR10 3DD – Eckington Wharf Picnic Place and car park, river left upstream of the bridge.

Description

Barely 300m after launching, **Pershore Lock** is reached on river left, opposite the gardens of the Angel Hotel and Star Inn; both establishments hired out boats to tourists in Pershore's Edwardian heyday. The Avon divides into four channels around the lock; the furthest river left is newly constructed (part of the Pershore Flood Alleviation Scheme), and leads around a barrier to a sluice and hydro-power station, a dead end. The next channel leads immediately to the brink of a sloping weir. The lock itself occupies the third channel, and the furthest river right (and furthest downstream) channel

Pershore Abbey.

Pershore Weir.

leads to another sluice at the former site of Pershore Mill (which burned down in 1976). Charles Showell judged the weir to be, *"the deepest and most dangerous on the river"* (*Shakespeare's Avon, from source to Severn*, 1901), although it's not clear what his white-water credentials were. It certainly isn't an inviting paddle, due to rocks along the base. The options for portaging are to carry past the lock, or to utilise gravity and lower boats downhill from the lock entrance and launch at the base of the weir.

Until 1972, the lock was visited by the Avon's last working freighter.

"Below Pershore Bridge there is trade on the river, most notably the up-to-date motor barge, Pisgah, which brings grain to Pershore Mill from Avonmouth, far down the Severn."

Robert Aickman in *Portraits of Rivers*, 1953

The two Pershore bridges – Great Bridge, then New Bridge – sit alongside one another, just outside town. The six sandstone arches of Pershore Great Bridge first spanned the Avon in the fourteenth century, since when it has enjoyed a colourful history! As one end belonged to Pershore Abbey and the other to Westminster Abbey, arguments about its upkeep meant that it was not well maintained. The Great Bridge was breached in 1644 by Charles I's army, retreating from Oxford to Worcester. The central arch suddenly collapsed during this demolition, killing 40 men. A week later, during Parliament's attempts to restore the crossing, *"the rest suddenly tumbled down, whereby about 60 workmen were knocked on the head or drowned"*. Today, the bridge's darker-coloured stone (from subsequent rebuilding) is the only clue to these appalling accidents. Note also the grooves in the sandstone, worn by generations of bargemen hauling their craft through.

A car park is squeezed between the bridges on river left, linked by a path passing under New Bridge to Pershore Bridges Picnic Place. Concrete Pershore New Bridge was built in 1928 to bypass the Great Bridge, which is now pedestrianised. Until 1956 there was also a watergate at this site, used to float boats upstream to Pershore Mill.

Note that at higher water levels, leisure boats can struggle to negotiate the two bridges; keep well clear!

Over the ten kilometres to Eckington Bridge, the Avon, *"writhes like a wounded snake"* (James Thorne, *Rambles by Rivers: The Avon*, 1845) with only one weir to break up the meanders. The saving grace is the lovely and ever-changing view of Bredon Hill, which grows closer and closer;

"... the protracted process of contemplating Bredon Hill along every possible line of sight. The river twists in and out upon itself, and every time it twists Bredon Hill looks so different that soon the navigator begins to distrust his memory."

Robert Aickman in *Portraits of Rivers*, 1953

Additionally, the Malvern Hills become visible to the west, and the Cotswold Hills line the south-east horizon.

Whenever the river switches course, it curves beneath steep wooded slopes on the outside of the bend. The right bend past the Pershore bridges leads below Pershore's horticultural college, and two kilometres further, a long left bend arcs beneath the bluebells of Tiddesley Wood, alongside moored boats at Defford

 *Pershore Bridges.*

◎ *Defford Road Wharf.*

Road Wharf. The third bend swoops right, below the village of Great Comberton.

Tiddesley Wood was the Abbot of Westminster's personal deer park until the dissolution. It's famous (well, mildly famous, locally) as in 1827 the landlord of the Butcher's Arms found a wild plum here, which he cultivated into the Pershore Yellow Egg Plum. This became wildly popular and a source of prosperity for Pershore, with 900 tons being picked and sold by the 1870s. Blink and you'll miss tiny Comberton Quay, tucked beneath trees on river left at the start of the third bend. Now a pleasure boat mooring, in 'ye olden days' corn was carted down steep Quay Lane from the village of Great Comberton and loaded here. It's a great spot for a picnic break, including a stroll up into the (predictably gorgeous) village.

One thing you'll notice about the houses hereabouts is the change to a honey-brown colour, and the appearance of drystone walls; Bredon Hill is an isolated outlier of the Cotswolds and this is the distinctive oolite limestone of those hills. Great Comberton and Bredon Hill are encompassed within the Cotswold Area of Outstanding Natural Beauty (AONB).

◎ *Great Comberton.*

Above Nafford Lock.

The real reason for landing at Great Comberton is that this is the best point from which to launch a Bredon Hill summit bid! Pass the fifteenth-century Church of St Michael and All Angels, with its four-pinnacled tower, and just keep going uphill. A footpath continues from the end of the road, clawing its way to the top after two thigh-burning kilometres.

Back along the river, no trace survives of Nafford village. It was mentioned in the Domesday Book, but Thomas Habington recorded that, *"Nafford lyeth now interred without a monument"* (*A Survey of Worcestershire*, 1640s); it seems that the village was at some point totally buried by a landslide! Nafford Mill was destroyed by fire in 1909 (the poor miller described it in the *Evesham Journal* as, *"alight from end to end and top to bottom"*) and hence **Nafford Lock** sits remote and isolated, a distinct change from the previous two busy lock complexes around Pershore.

"One of the most verdant spots on the Avon, but to call it a verdant spot does not express the depth and variety of its greenery ... between the waters are several small islands, edged with dark rushes and pale reeds, and covered with a luxuriant growth of osiers, nettles, docks and burdocks."

John Henry Garrett, *The Idyllic Avon* 1906

The main river left channel leads directly ahead to three large (deadly) sluice gates. The lock itself, crossed by a swing bridge, is somewhat hidden on a central channel between several islands. The lock can be portaged on the right-hand side. The best option, however, is to portage Nafford Weir (this is *not* the sluice gates). To reach the weir, peel off into the small river right channel which appears at the very start of the islands; there is a sign directing paddlers to this portage route, but it is easy to miss. This appealingly overgrown channel leads you to the brink of Nafford Weir and you need to hop out on river right, directly above. Naturally, this could be risky in high water, at which times the lock channel will be a safer bet.

Nafford Lock.

Nafford Weir is steeper and more channelled than other sloping weirs on the Avon Navigation, plunging directly beneath a footbridge into a vigorous stopper, divided by a central pillar. At certain levels the weir is noted by white-water paddlers as a half-decent play-spot, at other levels it can become a walled-in nightmare. Either way, the weir is a definite portage for anyone without understanding and experience of white water. Cross the footbridge and launch at the beach beside the weir pool.

Berwick Brook joins on river right at the weir pool, actually a tiny off-shoot of the Avon which departed the river a kilometre upstream. The swampy land enclosed by the brook is Gwen Finch Wetland Reserve, frequented by otters.

Nafford Weir mishap.

Eckington Bridge.

The channel leading back to the main river alongside Nafford Island (a bird reserve) is narrow, winding and tree-infested, great fun!

"... to Nafford it is even more beautiful; the river curves around to approach the old sandstone bridge at Eckington."

Noel Carrington and Patricia Cavendish, *Camping by Water* 1950

The last couple of kilometres to Eckington Bridge are pretty tortuous. A sharp right bend away from the hillside is soon followed by the aptly-named Swan's Neck. Here, the Avon executes a full 180-degree about-turn, so sharp a left bend that long barges struggle; beware! Birlingham Wharf is on the river right outside of the bend; if you follow the footpath from here to Birlingham village, check out St James' Church which has a weirdly pointed turret jutting from one corner of its tower.

Eckington Bridge is unmistakeable with its six irregular arches, a gnarled and ancient thing of sandstone beauty. Pass the moorings at Eckington Wharf on river left and take out just above the bridge at the car park, where the ice cream van will definitely be awaiting your arrival*.

*Disclaimer: there may not be an ice cream van awaiting your arrival.

Bredon Hill.

Bredon Hill

In summertime on Bredon ...
Here of a Sunday morning
My love and I would lie,
And see the coloured counties,
And hear the larks so high
About us in the sky.

A. E. Housman, *A Shropshire Lad* 1896

The 299m Bredon Hill dominates the Avon between Pershore and Bredon. The name is Celtic (hill-down), so 'Bredon Hill' means hill-hill-hill, and it rears 282m above the River Avon (river-river).

The summit is crowded with interest; the earthworks of an iron age hillfort encircle it (fifty battle-scarred skeletons were excavated here, with Roman coins pointing the finger of blame); the Bambury Stones are a hunk of oolite limestone shattered into smaller pieces, including the instantly-recognisable Elephant Stone (when the bells of Pershore Abbey strike midnight, it moves downhill to drink from the river); towering over all of this is Parson's Folly, an eighteenth century summer house and lookout, built to boost the hill from 961 feet to one thousand. What you really came for though, is the breath-taking views; the Mendips and Cotswolds to the south, the Malverns and Black Mountains to the west, and of course the valleys below.

"... *the valleys of the Avon and Severn lie before us like a carpet, the Avon glinting in the sun in the most unexpected places.*"

Charles Showell, *Shakespeare's Avon, from source to Severn* 1901

Tewkesbury Abbey.

Borough Mills.

Section 9

Eckington Bridge to the River Severn

Distance 14.4km
Start △ Eckington Bridge SO 922 423 / WR10 3DD
Finish ◯ Lower Lode, Tewkesbury SO 880 317 / GL20 5GL

Introduction

"From Bredon to Strensham Lock the river winds along between flowery and wooded banks. From Strensham Lock to Nafford it is even more beautiful; the river curves around to approach the old sandstone bridge at Eckington."

Noel Carrington and Patricia Cavendish, *Camping by Water*, 1950

Carrington and Cavendish described the river in reverse, heading upstream (they were canoe sailors, who are an odd bunch) but their words hold true. This engaging and varied paddle follows the Avon along its final scenic reaches through floodland pasture into Tewkesbury, where the River Severn is joined.

Launch points

Eckington Bridge SO 922 423 / WR10 3DD – Eckington Wharf Picnic Place and car park, river left upstream of the bridge.

Strensham Lock SO 915 404 / WR10 3BQ – limited roadside parking at the end of Mill Lane, giving direct access to Strensham Lock via a footpath.

Bredon (Little Meadow River Park) SO 921 372 / GL20 7LG – small public park and picnic area on river left with adjacent small parking area on Dock Lane.

Bredon (Fleet Lane) SO 905 365 / GL20 7EF – parking area on river left, at end of Fleet Lane, opposite Twyning Green launch point. Road unsurfaced and very rough.

Eckington Bridge.

Twyning Green SO 904 365 / GL20 6FL – picnic area with limited parking on river right, end of Fleet Road.

Tewkesbury (Shakespeare Court) SO 891 328 / GL20 5UP – slipway on river left of the Mill Avon, end of Shakespeare Court. Parking a short distance upstream at Back of Avon Car Park, free but restricted to two hours outside Sundays.

Lower Lode Inn SO 904 365 / GL19 4RE – river right on River Severn, end of Bishop's Walk. Only for patrons or with permission.

Tewkesbury (Lower Lode) SO 880 317 / GL20 5GL – Lower Lode Lane Picnic Area, small free car park on river left at confluence of Mill Avon and River Severn.

Description

"The bridge, six-arched, with deep buttresses, seemed as old as Avon itself. It is built of the red sandstone so common in the neighbourhood; but time has long since mellowed and subdued its colour to reflect the landscape's mood."

Arthur Quiller-Couch,
The Warwickshire Avon, 1892

Eckington Bridge is reputedly the oldest on the Avon. It has been around since at least 1440, although much of the present structure dates from 1729. The navigation channel is low and narrow, a challenge for leisure craft in high water.

Bow Brook joins a little way downstream on river right (flowing from Tiddesley Wood)

Defford Quay Marina.

and then the three high iron spans of Defford Railway Bridge are passed beneath, leading to the moored boats on river right at Defford Quay Marina. The river banks and surrounding landscape are open and exposed, which explains the presence of Arden Sailing Club, the first of several passed on this section. What this means for the paddler is that hereabouts the wind may not always be your friend; the prevailing south-westerlies can turn the whole trip into a bit of a grind.

All that said, the Avon has a final hill offering some shelter.

"At a sudden bend of the river Strensham Church appears on a considerable eminence. This building, on a nearer approach, affords, with the surrounding objects and the beautiful mill beneath on the bank of the Avon, a scene which equally invites the pencil of the artist, and the pen of the observant traveller."

Picturesque Views on the Upper, or Warwickshire Avon, Samuel Ireland, 1795

The church of St John the Baptist, high above on river right, overlooks the approach to **Strensham Lock**. Upper Strensham Mill (mentioned by Ireland) was demolished in the 1920s, but much of interest remains. A chain of islands stretches along the centre of the river for 500m, linked by footbridges and a footpath. Following the upper channel downstream, you encounter:

- The lock itself, on river left. Note the flood marks on the lock keeper's cottage, now a private residence. This redbrick Victorian building was bought by the Lower Avon Navigation Trust in

Strensham Lock.

1952 and restored from dereliction.
- Eckington Sluice, dangerous and to be avoided (it also contains actual crocodiles, viewable from the footpath above)*.
- Strensham Weir. This is sloping and paddleable, providing that the stopper isn't looking too clingy.
- Two 'death-on-a-stick' sluice gates.
- The end of the channel, on river right. The water passes beneath Old Eckington Mill House (powering a hydro scheme). If you follow the footpath down to here, you'll find that it actually passes through a gate in a wall into the back garden of this property!

It's possible to portage right at the start, along the river left bank of the lock. A potentially easier option is to paddle a short distance further, carefully passing Eckington Sluice, to a landing stage. From here you can portage across the island and launch into the channel below the lock and sluices.

The river left bank facing all of this glorious riverine heritage is glorious Andrew's Field campsite (literally a field, no facilities),

Strensham Weir.

* Some joker has placed fibreglass crocs in the channel, and genuine warning signs are posted up.

backed by glorious Bredon Hill. In case you're not picking up on the hints, this is a truly glorious spot. A lane leads inland from the field to reach the village of Eckington after a kilometre, where there are shops and couple of pubs. Almost tediously predictable, Eckington is yet another beautiful chocolate-box affair.

"... contains a number of quaint and pretty houses – chiefly thatched and half-timbered – which, scattered about in picturesque order in the midst of flowers and foliage, renders the village one of more than ordinary beauty and interest."

T.H. Packer, *Round Bredon Hill*, 1903

Below Strensham, the banks open out once more and if the wind is blowing, you will have to hug the reed and water lily-strewn shore of Bredon Ham (the flood-meadow on river right) for shelter. The Coventry Water Main (last seen near Wyre Piddle) curves overhead via a bridge and then the Severn Sailing Club is reached, on river left. Yes, you read that last bit right; and Avon Sailing Club is based on the River Severn! The Avon becomes the border between the counties of Gloucestershire (river right) and Worcestershire, while the needle-like 52m spire of Bredon's church, a local landmark, guides you further south:

"Then, hey for covert and woodland, and ash and elm and oak,
Tewkesbury inns, and Malvern roofs, and Worcester chimney smoke,
The apple trees in the orchard, the cattle in the byre,
And all the land from Ludlow town to Bredon church's spire."

London Town, John Masefield, 1923

 Bredon.

Tithe Barn at Bredon.

Bredon is reached where the river bends right, at islands lined by moored boats. The former site of Bredon Dock is recalled by Little Meadow River Park, a picnic spot on river left. Unlike most of the Avon's villages, which are obscured by trees or located back from the river, Bredon spreads along a sheltering slope, in full view. You'll already be well-acquainted with St Giles' Churches' spire. The church sits on the site of an Early Medieval monastery destroyed by Danes, c850. If you land to explore Bredon on foot (and you really should), note also the Elizabethan stone rectory, the seventeenth-century brick Old Mansion House and the eighteenth-century stone Manor House. There are in addition a few shops, but the real reason for landing is Bredon Barn, reached via a path through the churchyard.

"The great barn ... in its size exceeds the church or any other building in its vicinity. The tithe, or tax on the lands of the parish for the support of the church, originally consisted of one tenth of the produce, which was paid in kind, and these great tithe barns were built for the reception of the corn."

John Henry Garrett, *The Idyllic Avon*, 1906

This 40m-long tithe barn was built c1340 from oak and Cotswold stone, and has been restored after a 1980 fire. As Garrett describes, these barns were used to store produce surrendered to the church. Standing on the pigeon-shit-coated floor in the centre of this vast (even by modern standards) airy indoor space offers a good insight as to the surprising wealth of late medieval England, and also the churches' extraordinary power in divesting the populace of said wealth. See also, abbeys,

The M5 Bridge.

cathedrals and so forth. The barn is cared for by the National Trust and visitors are welcome to wander in, free of charge. Incidentally, there is a similar tithe barn beside the River Severn at Ashleworth, downstream of Tewkesbury. It had to cross the Avon somewhere and unfortunately Bredon drew the short straw; this lovely village suffers the presence of the M5 bridge, directly downstream. Paddle past quickly to reach Twyning Green. On river right, the Fleet Inn sits alongside a picnic area, whilst a very rough road leads to the river on the far bank. *Fleet* means 'float', or ferry; vehicles and livestock crossed here precariously.

Fleet Inn, Twyning Green.

"The stretch between Tewkesbury and Twyning Ferry is a fine sailing reach; the wind blows unchecked across the flat meadows here."

Noel Carrington and Patricia Cavendish, *Camping by Water*, 1950

The Avon flows for three kilometres directly south to Tewkesbury, with The Mythe forming the river right skyline; this low hill separates the Avon from the ever-closer River Severn (*Mythe*: Old English for 'river confluence'). The county boundary departs the river (you're now in Gloucestershire), and then the entrance to huge Tewkesbury Marina is passed on river left. The Avon now becomes as urban as it ever gets, briefly hemmed in by housing and tall warehouses ... and it's actually rather pleasant!

The girders of Bailey Bridge are passed beneath; this is disused and formerly carried a rail line. An enormous sluice gate on river right is followed by a vertically-falling weir, hidden from view beneath a barrier. The river right bank is now the island of Avon Lock, dividing the 'true' Avon from the Mill Avon, which you are now paddling.

"King John, being Earl of Gloucester by his wife, caused the bridge of Tewkesbury to be made of stone."

John Leland, *The Itinerary*, 1535–43

King John's Bridge is the final crossing of the Navigation, with four low arches. The highest gives just three metres of clearance, offset to the current; a challenge to leisure craft who will make a warning blast on their horn before squeezing below its arches. The original 'Long Bridge' commissioned c1205 by John I stretched 162m across both arms of the Avon; the bridge today has undergone too many rebuilds to list.

When you reach the entrance to **Avon Lock** on river right, you have a choice of routes to the finish at Lower Lode; either continue on the Mill Avon to the end (173.7km from the source) or portage Avon Lock (on its right-hand / north side) into the final 400m of the Navigation following the 'true' Avon and then follow the River Severn (300m longer overall).

📷 *King John's Bridge.*

◉ *Borough Flour Mills.*

The Mill Avon

The Mill Avon is an artificial channel, most likely engineered by the monks of Tewkesbury Abbey during the twelfth century. It offers a great little adventure to finish off your Avon journeys, exploring some of Tewkesbury's most lovely corners; but it does involve a potentially awkward portage.

Charles Showell described the scene downstream of Avon Lock, on the Mill Avon: *"forsaken wharves and warehouses of the past life of Tewkesbury, now mostly in ruins"*. He was right about this, but he also admitted that these buildings add, *"a certain amount of charm to the scene"* (*Shakespeare's Avon, from source to Severn* 1901).

Quay Street Bridge is a curved cast iron bridge which has crossed the Mill Avon since 1822. Towering above it is Borough Flour Mills, also known as Healing's Mill. Samuel Healing built this massive steam-powered complex in 1865. It was modified in the 1930s and 1970s, and closed down in 2006. Historic England's Grade II listed status notes that the mill is, *"an increasingly rare survival, a large-scale flour milling operation ... an architectural statement of some distinction"*. On the river left bank, also derelict, is Tewkesbury Brewery.

A curved footbridge crosses and the river leads between the old wharves on river left and the open meadows of Severn Ham, which open out on river right. Severn Ham is the island separating the Mill Avon from the River Severn, 72 hectares of common access meadow which floods annually. Ahead, the tower of Tewkesbury Abbey rears impressively over the houses of the regenerated riverfront. A slipway on river left offers the chance to explore Tewkesbury or finish the trip before the final weir.

There has been a mill on the site of Abbey Mill since at least 1190. The current redbrick edifice dates from 1793 and originally had four waterwheels. Framed by timber-framed buildings, warehouse buildings and a plunging vertical weir, not to mention the Abbey behind, it makes for a picturesque scene! Dinah Craik utilised the location as Abel Fletcher's Mill in her 1856 novel *John Halifax, Gentleman*.

The weir is blocked by a floating barrier and is not an inviting paddle in any case. Portage past the weir on river right, along a footpath. To get out and then back into the water, you will probably need to make use of the gaps in the reeds cleared for angling; exercise discretion and care. Below the weir, portage past the fencing before returning to the water. The Mill Avon below Abbey Mill is overgrown and ditch-like, a complete change of character! It winds among and through trees and bushes for the final 1.5km, the town and

Tewkesbury Abbey.

Abbey Mill, Tewkesbury.

The Mill Avon below Tewkesbury.

Severn Ham both hidden from view. The only landmark is the River Swilgate, dropping in from Bloody Meadow via a culvert on river left. The Bloody Meadow is the land between the Abbey and Mill Avon, the site of a massacre during the 1471 Battle of Tewkesbury; on this day the Avon was, *"Alas, a crimson river of warm blood"* (*Titus Andronicus*).

A final blind corner brings you, without warning, to the open expanse of the River Severn, exactly at the Lower Lode take-out.

The Avon and River Severn

If you choose to portage Avon Lock and follow the 'true' Avon to the end of the Navigation, this option is complicated by Upper Lode Lock on the River Severn. You also need a license to pass through the lock; see page 41.

Below Avon Lock, you'll get a glimpse on river right of Beaufort Bridge, the western half of King John's Bridge. Avon Lock's weir is further upstream past the bridge, if you want to go exploring. Otherwise, it's just 400m to the confluence with the River Severn; there is a spit on river right which leisure craft cutting the corner sometimes run aground upon, be aware that most will need to give this a wide berth.

"Here is the ultimate end of the Avon ... it flows softly into the Severn, surrendering itself without a commotion to the greater river. At this spot we stand awhile to contemplate the meeting of the waters ..."

John Henry Garrett, *The Idyllic Avon*, 1906

It might be the *"ultimate end"* of the Avon, but your trip isn't over ...

You have just 700m to adjust to the wider

The Battle of Tewkesbury

The Avon starts and finishes at the sites of climactic battles: Naseby (1645) and Tewkesbury (1471). The Battle of Tewkesbury was part of the Wars of the Roses, a vicious struggle for England's throne between the Houses of Lancaster and York. Yorkist King Edward IV faced Margaret of Anjou, wife of deposed Lancastrian King Henry VI. The Queen was defeated and her son Edward executed on the battlefield (he is buried in Tewkesbury Abbey). Retreating Lancastrian troops, cut off by the River Swilgate and Mill Avon, were massacred at (subsequently-named!) Bloody Meadow. Survivors who sought sanctuary in the Abbey were chased inside and hacked to bits; the Abbey had to be re-consecrated! Many more were executed at High Cross, the site today of the town's War Memorial. On Edward IV's return to London, Henry VI (a prisoner in the Tower of London) was murdered, to tie up loose ends. Shakespeare has Edward IV concluding,

"Once more we sit in England's royal throne,
Re-purchased with the blood of enemies."

Henry VI Part III

---

horizons and faster flow of the Severn, before an island is reached; this is Upper Lode Lock. The river left channel leads directly to a wide weir;

"We soon heard a sound of falling water, and proceeding very cautiously, we distinguished right ahead of us a mark across the river, which on our nearer approach, we found to be a weir with a heavy fall ... we congratulated ourselves on not having gone over it, as it looked very considerable."

Howard Williams, *The Diary of a Rowing Tour from Oxford to London*, 1875

Nowadays, a barrier gives warning. The sloping weir has a wide sticky stopper; runnable in low flows, but these are uncommon and getting out to inspect is awkward. It is similarly tricky to portage and this isn't really recommended. Incidentally, very large tides travel this far up the Severn (20km above the inland Port of Gloucester); there was a seal swimming in the weir's stopper during our last visit!

So, you need to follow the river right channel and negotiate Upper Lode Lock. The lock is almost impossible to portage, due to very high banks. The lock keeper (extremely helpful, in our experience) will give you directions as to how and when to enter the lock chamber. You'll need evidence of a license or British Canoeing membership and you may face a long wait, as paddlecraft are not allowed to share with powered craft (due apparently to risk from fumes). You'll spend around half an hour in the lock, it needs that long to drain! Howard Williams recorded, *"I had never*

📷 *Lower Lode.*

been in such an enormous lock before; the walls were quite 30 feet high" (*The Diary of a Rowing Tour from Oxford to London*, 1875). The lock is even larger than Williams experienced; the previous two chambers have been combined into one 92m-long amphitheatre, up to 24m wide. Sitting alone in a tiny paddlecraft at the heart of this utterly vast construction, engineered for ocean-going ships, feels both inspiring and rather silly.

Below Upper Lode Lock, it's just a kilometre to Lower Lode.

Variations

The River Severn offers attractive paddling both downstream to the tidal head at Maisemore and the Port of Gloucester and upstream to Upton-upon-Severn and beyond. The river is described in detail in the author's guidebook *Paddle the Severn*.

Tewkesbury

"Tewkesbury Abbey would alone be sufficient glory for any little town, but even without its abbey Tewkesbury would be very hard in its own style to find a match for anywhere."

Arthur Granville Bradley, *The Rivers and Streams of England*, 1909

Tewkesbury, which takes its name from an Early Medieval hermit called Theoc, is a gorgeous town. There are over 200 listed buildings in the centre (which is a conservation area), mostly half-timbered and overhanging with names such as 'House of the Nodding Gables'. Many are squeezed into narrow side streets which reward exploration, e.g., Baptist Chapel Court leads to a 1655-built chapel and burial ground. The Royal Hop Pole Inn on Church Street featured in Charles Dickens' *The Pickwick Papers*.

Samuel Rudder noted how Tewkesbury is, *"situated in a rich vale … watered by four rivers, like the garden of Eden"* (*A New History of Gloucestershire*, 1779). The convergence of the Severn, Avon, Swilgate and Carrant Brook at Tewkesbury explains the regular flooding (major floods in 1947, 1960, 1998, 2007…); a local saying "the water is out at Tewkesbury" means that Severn Ham is underwater. Tewkesbury also has a history of boatbuilding; a ship was built for Elizabeth I, a dozen 'Severn trows' (river barges) were launched between 1788 and 1855 and harbour defence motorboats were produced during the Second World War.

The town's historic affluence ensured that Tewkesbury Abbey became the best preserved of the Avon's abbeys; when Henry VIII's commissioners arrived in 1540 to dissolve the Abbey, £453 was raised to buy the church. This spectacular survivor originates from 1121, constructed from Bredon Hill limestone on the site of a previous monastery (burned down twice in the ninth century by marauding Danes). Pevsner called the 45m tower, *"probably the largest and finest Romanesque example in England"*.

Tewkesbury.

Launching at Pershore.

Launching on the Avon

"There is a tide in the affairs of men
Which, taken at the flood, leads on to fortune;
Omitted, all the voyage of their life
Is bound in shallows and in miseries.
On such a full sea are we now afloat,
And we must take the current when it serves."
                                    Julius Caesar

The Avon has a reasonable number of spots, spread along its length, from which to launch your paddlecraft. However, information about them has historically been hard to track down. Some launch points, even where public footpaths lead to the water at former ferry crossings, have seemingly been deliberately obscured or allowed to become inaccessible. Additionally, a number of locations where there is public access to the river bear warning signs from angling associations (sometimes many, many signs). These are aimed at warding off 'rival' anglers, but could (no doubt, entirely unintentionally) be misinterpreted as meaning that access is for anglers only. These factors have undoubtedly discouraged some paddlers from enjoying the river in the past.

The river sections in this book are designed to start and finish at launch points where accessing the water is reasonably simple (or is the least difficult of the various options!). In the case of the Avon Navigation, the sections start and finish at spots where there is space for larger groups, without the curse of height barriers.

The list below is by no means exhaustive, but hopefully offers a wide enough range of possibilities to give access to all sections. Unless a launch spot is indicated as being appropriate for larger groups, assume that there is only space, or it is only appropriate, for a handful of paddlers and one or two vehicles. Exercise discretion, act respectfully and ideally don't linger while changing or getting organised at these places; not because you aren't allowed to be there, but because you want to be welcomed back (many spots are in tiny villages, for example). Marinas have not been included, being geared towards larger craft. However, some may be willing to allow launching (for a fee), if approached.

It should be noted that not all spots listed are on public land; check details in the section description.

Launch points

Waypoint	Grid reference	Post code	Possible launch point?	Larger groups?	Distance from previous waypoint	Distance from source of Avon
Upper Avon						
Source of the Avon, Naseby	SP 688 782	NN6 6DF	N	N	0km	0km
Welford	SP 645 807	NN6 6JQ	N	N	6.7km	6.7km
Stanford Reservoir	SP 611 811	LE17 6DY	N	N	7km	13.7km
Stanford Hall	SP 587 788	NN6 6JP	N	N	3.8km	17.5km
Lilbourne	SP 559 775	CV23 0SX	N	N	4.6km	22.1km
Newbold on Avon	SP 490 770	CV21 1EF	Y, RR	Y	11.4km	33.5km
Bretford Bridge	SP 429 769	CV23 0LB	Y, RL	N	10.7km	44.2km
Wolston	SP 409 758	CV8 3HP	Y, RL/ RR	N	3km	47.2km
Citrus Hotel	SP 368 753	CV8 3DY	Y, RL	N	7.2km	54.4km
Bubbenhall	SP 360 725	CV8 3BE	Y, RL	N	4.6km	59km
Stare Bridge	SP 329 714	CV8 2LH	Y, RR	N	4.6km	63.6km
Ashow	SP 311 702	CV8 2LE	Y, RL	N	5.9km	69.5km

Waypoint	Grid reference	Post code	Possible launch point?	Larger groups?	Distance from previous waypoint	Distance from source of Avon
Chesford Bridge	SP 302 698	CV8 2LN	Y, RR	N	1km	70.5km
Hill Wootton Road	SP 309 691	CV32 6QN	Y, RL	N	1.3km	71.8km
St Nicholas Park	SP 288 647	CV34 4QY	Y, RR	Y	7.9km	79.7km
Barford	SP 267 609	CV35 8EH	Y, RL	N	5.5km	85.2km
Hampton Lucy	SP 257 571	CV35 8BA	Y, RR	N	7.8km	93km
Alveston	SP 236 565	CV37 7QX	Y, RL	N	3.5km	96.5km
Tiddington	SP 220 560	CV37 7AN	Y, RL	N	3.9km	100.4km
The Old Bathing Place	SP 209 557	CV37 0NS	Y, RR	Y	1.2km	101.6km
The Avon Navigation						
Stratford-up-on-Avon (Recreation Ground)	SP 204 546	CV37 7PY	Y, RL	Y	1.4km	103km
Binton Bridges	SP 099 517	B50 4AD	Y, RL	N	8km	111km
Bidford Bridge	SP 099 517	B50 4AD	Y, RL	Y	7km	118km
Marlcliff	SP 093 505	B50 4NT	Y, RL	N	1.5km	119.5km
Cleeve Prior	SP 079 498	WR11 8JZ	Y, RL	N	2.2km	121.7km
Offenham Weir	SP 065 470	WR11 8QT	Y, RL	N	3.5km	125.2km
Offenham	SP 049 457	WR11 8RS	Y, RL	N	3.3km	128.5km
Evesham (Waterside Gardens)	SP 038 434	WR11 1BU	Y, RL	Y	2.7km	131.2km
Evesham (Crown Meadow)	SP 035 432	WR11 4SS	Y, RR	Y	0.3km	131.5km

Waypoint	Grid reference	Post code	Possible launch point?	Larger groups?	Distance from previous waypoint	Distance from source of Avon
Evesham (Abbey Bridge)	SP 033 431	WR11 4BY	Y, RR	Y	0.3km	131.8km
Evesham (Hampton Ferry)	SP 029 436	WR11 4AF	Y, RR	Y	0.9km	132.7km
Fladbury (Fladbury Mill Meadow)	SO 996 459	WR10 2QA	Y, RR	N	7.4km	140.1km
Fladbury (Jubilee Bridge)	SP 000 456	WR10 3NG	Y. RL	Y	0.5km	140.6km
Wyre Piddle (beside Anchor Inn)	SO 965 474	WR10 2JB	Y, RR	N	5.4km	146km
Wyre Piddle (Smith's Meadow)	SO 961 473	WR10 2JD	Y, RR	N	0.6km	146.6km
Pershore (Avon Meadows Community Wetland)	SO 951 461	WR10 1EY	Y, RR	Y	1.6km	148.2km
Pershore (Recreation Ground)	SO 952 460	WR10 1EY	Y, RR	Y	0.1km	148.3km
Pershore (New Bridge)	SO 952 450	WR10 3NW	Y, RL	Y	1km	149.3km
Eckington Bridge	SO 922 423	WR10 3DD	Y, RL	Y	10km	159.3km
Strensham Lock	SO 915 404	WR10 3BQ	Y. RL	Y	3.2km	162.5km
Bredon (Little Meadow River Park)	SO 921 372	GL20 7LG	Y, RL	N	3.4km	165.9km
Bredon (Fleet Lane)	SO 905 365	GL20 7EF	Y, RL	Y	1.9km	167.8km
Twyning Green	SO 904 365	GL20 6FL	Y, RR	N	0km	167.8km
Tewkesbury (Shakespeare Court)	SO 891 328	GL20 5UP	Y, RL	Y	4.2km	172km
Tewkesbury (Lower Lode)	SO 880 317	GL20 5GL	Y, RL	Y	1.7km	173.7km
Lower Lode Inn	SO 904 365	GL19 4RE	Y, RR	Y	-	174km

Eckington Bridge.

Andrew's Field Campsite, Strensham.

Camping

"What could be more romantic than living in a tent by a mill on the Avon? ... having no thought whatever excepting for what you shall eat, though in regards to cooking and making of beds you are thrown upon your own resources. This, for a brief time, is delightful enough, even if a longer experience of it might tire."

John Henry Garrett, *The Idyllic Avon*, 1906

Camping beside water is just about the finest thing you can do with your life (apart of course from paddling *on* water). Rather splendidly, the Avon Navigation has a decent number of pleasant campsites along its banks from which to either base yourself or, given that they are helpfully spaced apart, plan a multi-day expedition around. It also has some large caravan and holiday parks, which may or may not be your thing. The Upper Avon is notably less well-served by campsite options, although there are still several appealing sites within a reasonable distance of the river.

There is no legally enshrined right to 'wild camp' in most of England. If this practice is something that you wish to learn more about, start by looking up the *Wild Camping Code of Conduct* online.

On the next page are listed campsites, hostels and 'glamping' options along or near the Avon. Most are closed over the winter months. Be mindful that campsite details change more regularly than any other aspect of this guidebook's information; campsites open, campsites close. Also, some of these sites get very busy and are booked up months in advance; you are strongly recommended to call ahead and check what is available before setting off!

Name	Number on maps	Section(s)	Grid reference	Post code	Beside river? (River right, river left)
Manor Farm	1	Source	SP 550 781	LE17 6DB	Y, RL
Hilltop Hideaways	2	2	SP 376 671	CV33 9EL	N, RL
Twitey's Tipis and camping meadows	3	3	SP 255 551	CV35 9EX	N, RL
YHA Stratford-upon-Avon	4	3, 4	SP 231 562	WR11 8PA	N, RL
Apple Farm	5	3, 4	SP 210 587	CV37 0QA	N, RR
Riverside Caravan Park	6	3, 4	SP 217 561	CV37 7AB	Y, RL
Stratford Racecourse Touring Park	7	4, 5	SP 185 539	CV37 9SE	N, RR
Weston Farm	8	5	SP158519	CV37 8JY	Y, RL
Pilgrim Lock	9	5	SP 120 516	CV37 8BA	Y, RL
Cottage of Content	10	5	SP 107 512	B50 4NP	Y, RL
Offenham Touring Park (Fish and Anchor Inn)	11	6	SP 065 470	WR11 8QT	Y, RL
Evesham Caravan Site	12	6	SP 042 440	WR11 4BX	Y, RR
Sankey Marine	13	7	SP 031 454	WR11 4TA	Y, RR
Plum Tree Glamping	14	7	SP 004 483	WR10 2NB	N, RR
Wyre Mill Club	15	7	SO 956 468	WR10 2JF	Y, RR
Andrew's Field	16	9	SO 915 404	WR10 3BG	Y, RL
Croft Farm Water Park	17	9	SO 907 354	GL20 7EE	N, RL
The Willows	18	9	SO 878 317	GL19 4RE	Y, RR
Lower Lode Inn	19	9	SO 879 317	GL19 4RE	Y, RR

Phone	Website/ email	Notes
01788 869002	www.manorfarmcatthorpe.co.uk	Not a paddleable section of the river!
07966 797474	www.hilltophideaways.com	900m from the Leam. Camping and glamping options
07725 944204	www.twiteystipis.co.uk	Camping and glamping options. 1km south of Charlecote Park
0345 371 9661	www.yha.org.uk	Youth Hostel in Alveston with glamping options, 400m from the river
07517 753777	www.theapplefarmsnitterfield.com	Camping and glamping options. 2km from the river, 3km from Stratford-upon-Avon
01789 292312	www.campingandcaravanningclub.co.uk	Camping and Caravan Club. Expensive caravan park with no camping, but glamping pods
01789 201063	www.stratfordtouringpark.com	500m from the river, outside Stratford-up-on-Avon
01789 750688	www.campingandcaravanningclub.co.uk	Camping and Caravan Club Certificated Site
01789 773593	www.campingandcaravanningclub.co.uk	Camping and Caravan Club Certificated Site beside Bidford Grange Lock
01789 772279	www.cottageofcontent.com	Behind the Cottage of Content pub
01386 442011	www.fishandanchor.co.uk	Behind the Fish and Anchor Inn beside Offenham Weir
07812 034455	www.eveshamcl.co.uk	At Gas Works Wharf beside Evesham Weir, happy to take camping paddlers
01386 442338	www.sankeymarine.com	Beside the marina
07725 339209	www.plumtreeglamping.co.uk	Glamping only, 1km from the river
01386 552079	www.wyremillclub.co.uk	Camping and Caravan Club Certificated Site. Adults only
07775 733506/ 07977 426419	www.avoncamping.weebly.com	Beside Strensham Lock. No facilities, just a tap
01684 772321	www.croftfarmwaterpark.com	Large holiday park around a lake, 500m from the river
07707 031828	chris@newandusedboat.co.uk	Behind the Lower Lode Inn. Opposite the end of the Mill Avon, on the River Severn
01684 293224	www.lowerlodeinn.co.uk	Beside the Lower Lode Inn. Opposite the end of the Mill Avon, on the River Severn

📷 *The actual William Shakespeare, at The Birthplace.*

Culture and Landscape: The Story of the Avon

"What's past is prologue"
                                The Tempest

The Avon's engaging story is writ large in the landscape through which it flows. It is worth pondering on the fact that the landscape that you experience whilst paddling is the culmination of many thousands of years of changes and developments – some gradual, some dramatic – yet it is not static and fixed in time, its story continues.

Geology

"O God, that one might read the book of fate
And see the revolution of the times
Make mountains level, and the continent,
Weary of solid firmness, melt itself
Into the sea."

                                Henry IV Part II

The Avon flows through a surface landscape laid down in the Quaternary Period (the ice ages of the last 2.5 million years to the present, barely registering on geological timescales). The valley is covered by glacial till (boulder clay) and also the deposits of ancient river systems; gravel, sand and clay.

Due to the generally low-lying nature of the region, the underlying rock (desert sands of the Triassic and, younger, shallow marine sediments of the Jurassic) is usually covered by these Quaternary deposits. A notable exception is the craggy outcrops of soft wind-blown Triassic sandstone along the Upper Avon at places like Guy's Cliffe, where it has been carved into caves. These cliffs are famed for

Guy's Cliffe Cloisters, carved from soft Triassic sandstone.

their fossil amphibians, first noted in 1842 by Richard Owen, the geologist who coined the term 'dinosaur'. The scarps of the Marlcliff and Cleeve Hill, lining the river downstream of Bidford-on-Avon, are formed of Triassic and Jurassic mudstone clays, which apparently proved shock-absorbent and able to, *"shrug off"* the Royal Engineers' explosions during the construction of Marlcliff Lock. Bredon Hill is topped by the (relatively young) Jurassic oolite limestone of the Cotswold Hills, visible in outcrops like the Bambury Stones and of course in the honey-coloured local buildings.

The course of the Avon

The Avon has only been a tributary of the Severn for a mere blink in geological time. A proto-Avon flowed *north* from Warwickshire to the Trent basin, around 500,000 years ago. Encroaching glaciers then barred the river's flow in all directions except south, where it was hemmed in by the Cotswold Hills. The result was 'Lake Harrison', a vast periglacial lake over 60m deep, submerging the Midlands from Warwick to Birmingham and Leicester, which persisted for around 10,000 years. As the ice sheets melted (around 424,000 years ago), the lake overtopped the land to the south-west and the Avon ground out its current course.

History

"It is alone among English rivers – perhaps among the rivers of the world. What scenes and men are before us! Naseby, Evesham, Tewkesbury, Stratford: Wiclif, Shakespeare, Butler. Places among the most celebrated in our history, and each, in the events connected with it, productive of large results. Men each among the notablest of his age and country – each embodying and giving expression to its thought – one the notablest of any age, and destined to shape the thoughts of men through many ages."

James Thorne,
Rambles by Rivers: The Avon 1845

The Avon quite literally flows through history; the story of our past is written in the landscape of battlefields, castles, abbeys and mills lining its banks. Also, of course, the man described above by Thorne as *"the notablest of any age"* lived hereabouts!

Prehistory to the Romans

Along the Avon, records of our early history are sparse. 500,000-year-old elephant bones and four handaxes were discovered at a quarry pit near Bubbenhall in the 1980s, among the earliest signs of Britain's colonisation by humans. Probably the most visible later prehistoric remains along the Avon are found

📷 *Evesham Bell Tower.*

around Bredon Hill, which is dotted by several standing stones and three separate Iron Age hillforts. Roman roads such as the Icknield Way and Fosse Way crossed the river (leaving traces of their engineering work in the riverbed at Bidford-on-Avon) and the Lunt Roman Fort is a reconstructed army camp beside the River Sowe near Coventry, several kilometres north of the Avon. The Romans also seem to have introduced waterwheels to the Avon.

The Middle Ages

The Early Medieval* period saw the Avon valley flourish into a region of immense wealth. The three great abbeys of Tewkesbury, Evesham and Pershore were all founded along the lower river between 681AD and 715AD (Stoneleigh came later, in 1154). Religious houses weren't just created to bring Christianity to the pagan locals, they served as regional economic powerhouses to manage, and profit from, the resources of the land and river. Fish weirs and mills proliferated along the river (in 1086, the *Domesday Book* listed 5,624 mills south of the River Trent) and the floodplain's rich fecundity was exploited by intensive farming. Further evidence of the church's wealth and power is demonstrated by the enormous tithe barns which survive at Middle Littleton and Bredon; these were warehouses for piling up the crops involuntarily surrendered by lay people.

*Previously (inaccurately) labelled, the 'Dark Ages' and more recently the 'Anglo-Saxon' period, however the latter term is becoming problematic due to US white supremacist connotations.

"Inseparable from the story of the Avon is that of the three great monasteries upon its banks, from the legends associated with their inception in Saxon times down to the great power they became in the West Midlands prior to their fall in the Dissolution."

Arthur Granville Bradley,
The Rivers and Streams of England 1909

Tithe Barn at Middle Littleton.

The Avon wasn't immune from Later Medieval England's political struggles. The Midlands saw a number of over-powerful nobles emerge to challenge the authority of the crown; Earl of Leicester Simon de Montfort lead the opposition to Henry III in the Second Baron's War, culminating in Montfort's defeat (and dismemberment) at the Battle of Evesham in 1265. Earl of Warwick Richard Neville's wealth and military strength, centred on Warwick Castle, contributed to the instability of the Wars of the Roses; he helped depose two kings and earned the title 'Kingmaker'. Warwick was killed at Barnet in 1471; the Battle of Tewkesbury, fought later that year, was bloodily decisive enough to put the conflict between the Houses of Lancaster and York on hold for the next fourteen years.

Warwick Castle.

📷 *Charlecote Park.*

📷 *The Gower Memorial, Stratford-upon-Avon.*

The Early Modern era

The Dissolution of the Monasteries dramatically changed the Avon's landscape. This was a greedy asset-grab by Henry VIII, dressed up as moralistic reform. Henry's Secretary Thomas Cromwell encouraged reports of sinful behaviour, and Pershore Abbey monk Richard Beerley duly obliged in a letter: *"The religion that we do observe and keep is no rule of Saint Benedict, nor is it no commandment of God, nor of no saint, but lies and foul ceremonies ... Monks drink a bowl after lunch until ten or twelve o'clock, and come to Matins as drunk as mice, some playing at cards, some at dice"*. These reports were used to justify dissolving all religious houses by 1540. Their possessions were confiscated; this included a third of all land in England! 74 parchment skins were needed to itemise Tewkesbury Abbey's treasures. Estates such as Stoneleigh Abbey were sold off to Henry's nobles. Monastic buildings were often demolished, but Evesham, Pershore and Tewkesbury Abbeys were each partially rescued by townsfolk raising money to buy the church buildings.

The following period of comparative peace saw the 'Great Rebuilding', when the nobility commissioned luxurious new mansions such as those lining the Avon at Charlecote Park, Stoneleigh Abbey and later, Stanford Hall. Crumbling castles like Warwick were converted into comfortable homes.

Amidst these wider social and political changes, the life of William Shakespeare (1564-1616) played out; he lived and worked between his hometown of Stratford-upon-Avon and London, prominent as a playwright in the reigns of Tudor and Stuart monarchs Elizabeth I and James I. The Bard of Avon's impact on the culture and landscape of the Avon was probably negligible in his lifetime, yet he was of course to become indivisibly associated with both the river and English identity.

"This blessed plot, this earth, this realm, this England."

Richard II

The English Civil War, fought between King Charles I and Parliament, very much left its mark on the Avon's landscape. The opening

📷 *Cromwell Memorial, Naseby.*

Battle of Edgehill (1642) was fought just southeast of Stratford and the Battle of Naseby (1645), which shattered Charles' army, was fought at the river's source!

'Nor had any river in England more concern with the great war between King and Parliament ... Naseby and Edgehill, as we have seen, were both fought upon or near its banks. But they were almost as nothing compared with the constant skirmishes and minor sieges, the burning and harrying that for four years went on along the banks'

Arthur Granville Bradley,
The Rivers and Streams of England 1909

The physical barrier formed by the river proved pivotal, and bridges along the Avon were repeatedly fought over. Evesham was a Royalist strongpoint, linking the King's bases at Oxford and Worcester; before it was captured in the Second Battle of Evesham (1645), the Royalists demolished the bridge twice! Bullet holes can still be seen in Evesham's Bell Tower. Clopton Bridge at Stratford had an arch demolished, and traces of the damage at Pershore Bridge can also be seen today.

The Industrial Age
The Avon Navigation

Although the Avon was the first river in Britain to be made navigable by pound locks, its development and use as a Navigation – a waterway transport network artificially engineered to serve industry and trade – has been a prolonged and tortuous process.

In the early fifteenth century the Earl of Warwick, *"was mynded to have made passage* for boattes from Tewkesbury to Warwick for tranportyng of merchaintdise for the advantage of Warwick", but nothing came of this until 1635 when;

"Wm Sandys of Fladbury in the County of Worcestershire, Esq, had undertaken at his own costs to make the River of Avon passable for boats of reasonable burthen from Severne where that river falls near Teuxbury ... unto or near the City of Coventry ..."

Houses of Parliament 1635

Sir William Sandys spent over £20,000 dredging the river and building locks. By 1639 the new Avon Navigation extended upstream from Tewkesbury to Alveston, but then the Civil War intervened.

"the said Mr Sandys imployed much time and expence to advance the work to Stratford-upon-Avon, which is above halfe the way to our said Citty of Coventry; and had then proceeded to finish to the same had not the supervening troubles of the nation interrupted him."

Thomas Habington,
A Survey of Worcestershire 1640s

Hence, the Navigation was not completed upstream to Warwick and Coventry as planned (and never has been since).

Ownership of the Navigation rights passed through various hands over the following centuries. In 1717, the Navigation was divided into the Upper and Lower Avon Navigations, with Evesham being the dividing point. A 1751 Act of Parliament confirmed the right of all to travel on the river (tolls not withstanding), *"The said River Avon shall forever thereafter*

Perrott House, Pershore.

be accounted and be a free river". The Lower Avon Navigation was bought by George Perrott in 1759, who was surprised to find the Navigation in a poor state and had to spend £4,000 restoring it.

Competition increasingly infringed on trade and profits; firstly, from the Stratford-upon-Avon Canal (completed in 1816) and then from the expanding railway network. The Oxford, Worcester and Wolverhampton Railway linked to Stratford, completed in 1853. The railway company purchased* the already-dilapidated Upper Avon Navigation in 1860, not to restore it, but ...

"... in order to abolish the competition of water-carriage with the railway. Having purchased this property, the company deliberately allowed it to fall into decay."

John Henry Garrett, The Idyllic Avon 1906

Tolls were not collected, removing the obligation to maintain the river. By 1873, only the steam barge *Bee* still made the journey from Gloucester to Stratford and by 1875, the Upper Avon Navigation was unnavigable.

In 1924 the Perrotts sold up to the Lower Avon

---

*Via legally dubious machinations involving the railway manager purchasing the Navigation in his own name.

Navigation Company Ltd, which tried and failed to save the lower river from also falling into ruin. By the time of the Second World War, the Avon was unnavigable above Pershore.

The post-war story of restoration is remarkable, all funded by public subscription and powered by volunteer work.

Douglas Barwell acquired the Lower Avon Navigation for £1500 and in 1950 formed the Lower Avon Navigation Trust. The Trust restored eight locks between Tewkesbury and Evesham by 1964, making the Avon navigable as far upstream as Offenham.

The southern part of the Stratford-upon-Avon Canal was restored by the National Trust in 1961-64, creating pressure to restore the link between Stratford and Evesham. The Upper Avon Navigation Trust was formed in 1965 and commenced restoring or replacing the remaining locks, as well as dredging the silted-up riverbed. The newly restored Upper Avon Navigation was opened by the Queen Mother in 1974; she arrived by helicopter and travelled by narrowboat through Stratford Trinity Lock into Stratford.

Schemes have been mooted since the 1980s to complete William Sandys' plans by extending the Navigation upstream to Warwick (the 'Higher Avon Navigation'). These have faced stiff opposition from landowners and from environmental advocates, such as the Warwickshire Wildlife Trust. In 2010, the two Navigation Trusts merged to form the Avon Navigation Trust, the non-profit-making charitable authority who currently maintain the Navigation.

Paddling the ruinous Avon

Prior to restoration, the Avon's locks were either blocked or had collapsed into dangerous cataracts. All accounts of paddling or rowing the river mentioned the challenges presented by the locks.

"The Avon presents some awkward problems ... in places locks and weirs have been partially removed, others have broken down, and nasty obstacles in the form of tumbledown masonry obstruct the channel in parts."

Alec R. Ellis, *The Book of Canoeing* 1935

William Bliss recalled Evesham Lock: *"It was just alive when I first came in 1891, but could only be opened by some extraordinary contrivance of derricks and pulleys and winches that looked exactly like one of Mr Heath Robinson's pictures"* (*The Heart of England by Waterway* 1933).

Trade and transport

In the eighteenth century, about 400 trows and barges plied the Navigation. Trows (rhymes with 'crows') were flat-bottomed barges with square sails and single lowerable masts, steered by a single oar. Medieval bridges at Tewkesbury, Eckington and Pershore, with only 2.5 metres of headroom, restricted the size of trows to around forty tons. When there was no wind, vessels were dragged upriver by teams of men;

"The navigation is conducted in a primitive fashion. Horses were not employed to draw the barges at first, nor are they now. At a huge

heavy-laden craft five or six men may be seen tugging laboriously; a miserable service for human beings to be put to ... it is a painful sight to see those men dragging their barge along this river which from its many curves would be extremely hard work for horses."

James Thorne,
Rambles by Rivers: The Avon 1845

In the nineteenth century, steam-powered barges came to predominate the river traffic.

"The river is an exceeding advantage to all this part of the country and also to the commerce of the City of Bristol. For by this river they derive a very great trade ..."

Daniel Defoe, *A Tour Through the Whole Island of Great Britain* 1725

The river trade revolved around coal being brought upriver (from Shropshire, on the Severn) and Midlands produce being sent downriver:

"Large quantities of coals were brought up the River Avon and landed at Evesham and Stratford ... and great quantities of corn and grain were brought down from the county of Oxford to Evesham and Stratford and there and at other mills ground into flour and sent down the river to Bristol and other places up and down the Severn ..."

George Perrott, *Journal of the House of Commons* 1769

Some idea of the range of transported goods can be gleaned from the 1751 *Act of Parliament* which fixed tolls, *"For every Ton of Cast or Pig-Iron, Brick, Stone, Lime, Coopers, Carpenters, Wheelwrights and other Timbers, Boards, and Firewood ... For every Wey of Wheat, Barley,*

The first ever steamboat?

In 1736, Gloucestershire farmer Jonathan Hulls applied for a patent for a ship powered by steam: *'a Newly Invented Machine for Conveying Vessels or Ships out of or into any Harbour, Port or River, Against Wind and Tide'*. He tested a prototype on the Avon at Evesham the following year, but it failed in front of a large crowd. The feedback was brutal:

Jonathan Hull
With his paper skull
Tried to make a machine
To go 'gainst wind and stream
But he, like an ass
Couldn't bring it to pass

Hull passed into obscurity and it was over half a century before his radical idea became a reality.

Malt, Beans, Peas, Oats, Masline, Linseen, Cutling, Clover, Meal and Flour ..."

Leisure and tourism

Stratford-upon-Avon established itself early as a destination for culture and 'Bardolatry', following David Garrick's 1769 Jubilee (see page 92).

With the decline of trade and industry on the Avon in the late nineteenth century, the river became the focus of leisure and a draw for visitors. The railways opened up 'Shakespeare Country', commencing a tourism boom which lasted through to the Second World War.

Working people from Birmingham (known as 'Dudleys') made excursions on Bank Holidays and weekends. Some were 'gongoozlers', barge slang for folk who just sat and watched the river. Many wished to experience the Avon more directly, and various entrepreneurs catered to this desire. Boat tours were a highlight of any visit; cruises ran from Bidford-on-Avon to Cleeve Mill and four pleasure boat companies operated from Evesham, with steamers transporting tourists to Fladbury and back. Holland's Pleasure Grounds at Bidford-on-Avon hired out punts and Canadian canoes; E. Davis at Stratford also offered new-fangled Rob Roy kayaks, launched from the Ferry Boat House beside the theatre. Those with affluence, and time spare to explore further, could hire a canoe or kayak and descend the whole river to Tewkesbury, as recommended by Edward J Burrow in his guidebook: *"The journey is inexpensive, for nowhere are the charges excessive either for hire of boat or lodging, and in some cases they are surprisingly low"* (*The Avon Valley*, 1901). Trip accounts from this era consistently complain about the physical barriers to their progress encountered at Charlecote Park and Warwick Castle, where the nobility had attempted to bar the public from the river. Howard Williams actually had

Evesham Lock.

to seek out the Earl of Warwick's steward and metaphorically doff his cap;

"He gave us the required permission, simply asking us a few questions as to where we had started from, and so on, to make sure that we were Bona Fide travellers, and not from Birmingham."

Howard Williams, *The Diary of a Rowing Tour from Oxford to London* 1875

Since the post-war restoration of the river, the focus of leisure has shifted to powered leisure boats, privately owned or hired; narrowboats up to 21 metres in length, and (in the lower reaches especially), plastic flat-bottomed 'broads cruisers'. By the early twenty-first century, over 10,000 journeys were made annually. Kayak and canoe clubs have also proliferated along the river, and it has been a focal point in particular for canoe slalom and marathon competitions.

Q at Eckington Bridge

Sir Arthur Quiller-Couch (known by the pen-name 'Q') was a writer and Shakespeare scholar. His account of a Victorian-era canoe trip down the length of the Avon is worth seeking out (it can be found online). Eckington Bridge inspired him to contemplate human history and the passage of time ...

"As we rested our elbows on the parapet, we noticed that many deep grooves or notches ran across it. They were marks worn in the stone by the tow-ropes of departed barges. Those notches spoke to us, as nothing had spoken yet, of the true secret of Avon. Kings and their armies have trampled its banks from Naseby to Tewkesbury, performing great feats of war; castles and monasteries have risen over its waters; yet none of them has left a record so durable as are these grooves where the bargemen shifted their ropes in passing the bridge."

Arthur Quiller-Couch,
The Warwickshire Avon 1892

Q concluded, *"It was a time, I think, that will pleasantly come back to us in days when we shall fear to trust our decrepit limbs in a canoe"*. Decades later, he did indeed revisit this experience:

"Man shall outlast his battles. They have swept

Avon from Naseby Field to Savern Ham;

And Evesham's dedicated stones have stepp'd

Down to the dust with Montfort's oriflamme.

Nor the red tear nor the reflected tower

Abides; but yet these elegant grooves remain,

Worn in the sandstone parapet hour by hour

By labouring bargemen where they shifted ropes;

E'en so shall men turn back from violent hopes

To Adam's cheer, and toil with spade again".

Arthur Quiller-Couch,
Upon Eckington Bridge, River Avon 1921

Eckington Bridge.

Avon at Stratford.

Wildlife and Environment

"The river moves beneath a breath
Of mists that swirl and whirl and eddy
In currents of a faery book.
Dark descends, and the trees retreat into the pillow of the soft black night.
Banks fade within the breathing silence
And the river is a long glass road
Cutting the velvet of the sleeping fields
And chuckling elfishly beneath the boat ..."

River, Richard Spender, 1942

Spender was a Stratford-upon-Avon local who was killed in North Africa in 1943, aged 21; *River* was composed a long way from the Avon, in a very different landscape.

The Avon is a beautiful natural environment. It is possible to paddle for hours, accompanied by birdsong, along a peaceful aisle of greenery with few signs of human development and only occasional traffic. Even in the few riverside towns, nature is ascendant along the riparian corridor. The river acts as an important wildlife highway for the region's flora and fauna, providing and connecting natural habitats within an otherwise intensively farmed landscape. The Midlands' diversity of plants, invertebrates, fish and birds is strongly dependent upon the health of the Avon.

It is important to understand however, that the stunning natural environs which you paddle among do not always tell a story of natural harmony or even good health. The river's wildlife and environment has faced, and continues to face, a range of serious challenges.

Environmental issues
The Navigation

Since the Avon Navigation was restored between the 1950s and 1970s (and all through the river's navigation history), there has been an inherent dilemma between the river's roles as an engineered navigation and a natural environment. The Avon Navigation Trust view their restoration of the Navigation as having saved and preserved its natural environment, although their explanation is somewhat contradictory.

"The river, as always, is striving to revert to her natural state – a muddy brook in summer and a raging torrent in winter. Only by maintaining weirs and locks and keeping channels dredged can she be preserved for the benefit of man and the environment."

The River Avon – *Navigation and Visitor Guide*, Avon Navigation Trust, 2014

Naturalists take a more circumspect view of engineering the Avon, *"for the benefit of man"*. They point to the significant reduction, or destruction, of habitat diversity and ecological value caused by straightening, widening and dredging the watercourse, by deepening the river with artificial weirs and by construction of moorings and marinas.

Pollution

Researching this book, the author uncovered an environmental report on the Avon, dated 1971. A map shaded the entire Upper Avon (and tributaries) as, 'badly polluted' and the Avon Navigation as 'dubious'. The report noted, *"... unpleasant odours, foaming and excessive growth of algae and water weeds ..."* and concluded that the river was, *"... unable to support a healthy fish population until some distance downstream from Warwick"*. The Rivers Sherbourne and Sowe in Coventry* were identified as the main culprits, where treated sewage

Freshwater mussel found on the riverbank.

was discharged directly into the water. Further pollution came from agricultural run-off.

Pollution reduces the oxygen saturation in a river; in the Upper Avon, it was well below 50%. Urban sewage and agricultural run-off caused severe eutrophication, the process whereby a high level of nutrients develops in a river. Algal blooms cover the surface and shut out light; the more eutrophicated a river, the less species diversity. Another concern was the use of organo-chlorine insecticides. Through the 1970s and 80s, high levels of this agricultural poison were detected in dead eels and herons; the otters *all* died.

The modern picture is (thankfully!) vastly improved, but far from perfect. In 2015, a survey of the 91 rivers in the Avon catchment rated them on number and diversity of fish, oxygen levels and degree of eutrophication. 18% were rated 'good', 18% 'poor' and the remainder (including the Avon itself) 'moderate'. Most of the water quality improvements have come over the last decade, EU legislation having had a major impact. Evidence of cleaner water can be seen in the water crowfoot growing in

---

*Having grown up alongside the Sherbourne in the 1970s, the author can vouch for its then-sorry state.

shallows, the freshwater mussels in the pools below some weirs and most spectacularly, the return of otters to all parts of the Avon.

Invasive species

The cleaner Avon has unfortunately helped facilitate the proliferation of non-native invasive species. Japanese knotweed grows fast, reaching nearly three metres in height, efficiently colonising new sites along the riverbank; it is unmistakeable by its large triangular leaves, red zigzag stems and spikes of white flowers near the leaf base in late summer. Himalayan balsam has large purple flowers, with explosive seed capsules that help it spread rapidly.

Non-native fish in the river include carp and zander. North American mink helped to decimate vole populations. Signal crayfish (escaped from farms in the 1970s) are bigger and more aggressive than our native white-clawed crayfish, causing a decline in the latter; the good news is that otters find them tasty.

Other intruders include the demon shrimp and killer shrimp. Yes, those really are their names.

Other issues

Excessive water abstraction has been a concern in the past. This is monitored by the Environment Agency, but the Vale of Evesham and other intensely farmed areas along the river continue to make high demands for irrigation. Physical barriers such as weirs reduce biodiversity, especially in the Avon's headwaters. Removing these from the smaller tributaries has been a key focus in recent years. On the Avon itself, fish and elver passes have been added to some weirs.

Housing and other commercial developments continue to encroach upon the Avon. Floods such as those in 2007 have clearly demonstrated the folly of building along the Avon's floodplain (5,000 properties inundated in Gloucestershire alone), but proposals continue. At the time of writing, Shakespeare Marina is being constructed at Stratford, and the HS2 railway is scouring out a shocking swathe of destruction right across the Upper Avon.

Habitats

Naturalists accept that the river will never return to a fully natural state. They are most concerned about, and preoccupied with, loss of habitat *diversity*; trying to preserve or restore a range of different natural habitats, to prevent the Avon's environment from becoming a monoculture of agricultural land, concreted moorings and groomed private gardens. Habitat diversity has largely been preserved on the Avon Navigation, albeit at times artificially. The Upper Avon preserves much greater habitat diversity. The Wildlife Trusts have strongly opposed proposals to complete the Navigation upstream to Warwick, noting for example that the Upper Avon would lose the river's fast-flowing shallow riffles and deep pools, home to over 200 species of plant. Outlined below are some of the Avon's classic habitats. Of course, these habitats aren't found in isolation; they physically overlap one another and are interconnected and interdependent.

Water meadows

"When daisies pied and violets blue,
And lady smocks, all silver-white,
And cuckoo-buds of yellow hue,
Do paint the meadows with delight".

Love's Labour's Lost

Water meadows are any grasslands alongside a river, but strictly speaking the term refers to land which is seasonally flooded, also known as flood meadows or 'damp meadows'. These meadows are usually managed environments with controlled irrigation to increase agricultural productivity. Traditional 'ham' water meadows, where the use of modern practices such as fertilisers is limited, have largely disappeared, so those along the Avon such as Upham Meadow and Severn Ham are precious environments; their fertile alluvium grasslands supporting populations of breeding and over-wintering birds such as redshank, curlew, snipe and lapwing.

Riverbanks

"I know a bank where the wild thyme blows,
Where oxlips and the nodding violet grows,
Quite over-canopied with luscious woodbine,
With sweet musk-roses and with eglantine".

A Midsummer Night's Dream

The Avon retains a diverse range of riverbank habitats. Dredging has created steep banks, which allow kingfishers and sand martins to dig out well-protected nest tunnels. Martins require large areas of bare bank to burrow fresh tunnels annually, as the old ones become cluttered with debris; an example of a sand martin 'city' can be seen on the river left side of the Mill Avon.

Shallow banks have emerged where silt has been deposited on the inside of bends. These are usually lushly overgrown, although the eutrophic conditions mean that only a relatively narrow range of plants are present. These marginal plants include colonies of meadowsweet (tall with creamy fragrant flower heads), purple-loosestrife (tall with purple flowers), and yellow iris (also called 'yellow flag', tall with flowers 100mm across, the 'flag').

Wetlands

Wetlands are any areas which are usually inundated by shallow water. The Avon has few extensive wetlands left (the largest, such as Brandon Marsh SSSI, are artificially created), mostly the wetland habitat is restricted to a strip along the water's edge. Approaching 90% of the UK's wetlands and half of its reedbeds have been lost since 1945. Preserving the Avon's wetlands is essential; aside from their role as a habitat, they capture carbon, store floodwater and filter out pollutants.

Rushes (true bulrush) and reeds (common reed and bur-reed) extend out into water up to a metre in depth. They shelter vulnerable water voles, are home to reed warblers and provide roosting sites for swallows and sand martins.

Yellow water-lily has colonised the outer margins of the reedbeds, instantly recognisable by the floating pads and yellow flowers. It's known as 'brandy bottle', due to its odour and

📷 *Reeds and lilies.*

bottle-shaped flowering heads. This native plant is common on the Avon, but not the River Severn.

Wet woodlands

*"And in the woods where you and I
Upon faint primrose beds were wont to lie."*

A Midsummer Night's Dream

Wet woodlands are found on poorly drained or seasonally flooded soils. Due to the difficulty of accessing or exploiting these secretive spots, they can be some of our most untouched and natural woodlands. The Avon's wet woodlands are often 'carr'; this term refers to low-canopied and tangled growths of birch, willow and alder which have established themselves over marshy tussocks of sedges, yellow iris and meadowsweet.

The water beneath is often choked with dead wood, important for insects. These secret habitats are hidden along the Avon in side channels, the backs of islands and the sites of former locks; the closest thing to mangrove swamps in the Midlands!

In the water

The Avon and many of its tributaries flow over Lower Lias clays, making it a eutrophic clay stream. This means that the river naturally has a high level of nutrients, leading to relatively low species diversity. As noted earlier, eutrophication is also caused (more severely) by pollution. Additionally, the water on the Avon Navigation is artificially deepened by dredging and is turbid / murky from passing powerboats (although traffic is lighter than on other

Navigations, such as the River Thames). The result of all these factors is that light struggles to reach the riverbed, hence plants don't grow mid-stream, hence a lack of in-stream habitat, hence reduced carrying capacity for fish and other species. Despite this, the river is heavily fished for its populations of barbel, bream, carp, chubb, dace, eels, perch, pike, roach, tench and zander (the latter introduced from Eastern Europe).

Wildlife

"One touch of nature makes the whole world kin".
Troilus and Cressida

A few of the Avon's star species are outlined below.

Otters

Otters have returned to all parts of the Avon! The Environment Agency's national survey in 2010 found, *"a major expansion of otter range in this catchment"* and concluded that these beautiful, sleek hunters, *"are now using the whole of the Rivers Severn and Avon and many of their tributaries"*. Their numbers were still low relative to many other regions of England; the population of Warwickshire has been estimated at around a dozen. Wildlife Trusts have worked to provide habitats to aid their passage; they are now well-established at places like Brandon Marsh and Gwen Finch Wetland Reserves, although an individual will range up to 40km along the river. You are unlikely to spot one whilst paddling in daytime, but vigilance at dusk or dawn might just pay off. Their spraint (dung) can often be spotted riverside, for example below weirs. It's recognisable as a 3–10 cm sweet-smelling turd, with scale and fish bones visible.

Water voles

Water voles were populous along the Avon, due to its ideal habitats of slow-moving water, reedbeds to hide among and steep overgrown banks in which to burrow their nest chambers. They are about 200mm long with a 100mm tail, distinguishable from rats and other mammals by their fluffy chestnut-brown fur, furry tails and small rounded ears. A number of factors (especially predation by minks) lead to their population crashing by 95%; they are the UK's most endangered mammal. Work is underway to support their ongoing recovery; one factor helping this is that the returning otters are displacing the minks.

Damselflies and dragonflies

These vividly colourful insects are easily spotted, flitting along the margins of the Avon's slow-moving waters. The flying creatures are just the final stage of their life cycle; their eggs are laid at the water's edge, they hatch into their larval state (in which they live in the water) and finally they crawl onto reeds or lily pads to undergo partial metamorphosis into adult fliers. How to tell them apart? Dragonflies are chunkier, have short bodies and keep their wings outstretched. Damselflies have extremely long and narrow bodies and fold their wings back.

Willows

"The Avon ... gathers about it a fine wealth of foliage, often stealing for long periods between screens of drooping alder and willow; avenues of verdure quivering again in the glassy depths."

Arthur Granville Bradley,
The Rivers and Streams of England, 1909

Willows spread their seeds efficiently and abundantly on the wind, and grow quickly once established on a riverbank. The 'weeping willow' is of course the most easily recognised; those which have sprung up alongside the abandoned Borough Flour Mills in Tewkesbury are a favourite of the author. However, the 'weeping willow' is non-native, only introduced to Britain in the eighteenth century.

Two native species are integral to the Avon; osier willows and crack willows. Osier willows are recognisable by their narrow leaves and often mark the sites of former osier beds, where they were cultivated on an industrial scale; one such site can be found on the islands at Strensham Lock. Osiers were pollarded (cut back to encourage growth) every 10–20 years, their pliable wood used to weave baskets. Crack willow has oval leaves and was also pollarded, its more brittle wood utilised for fencing.

Birds

"Avon is alive with moorhen and sandpiper and dabchick and heron, and sometimes kingfishers, and every kind of water bird."

William Bliss,
The Heart of England by Waterway, 1933

Outlined below are some of the author's favourites. Other commonly encountered birds include cormorants, greylag geese, little egret, little grebe, sand martin, warblers and a whole panoply of additional species, dependent upon the location and habitat.

Coots and moorhens

Coots and moorhens are commonly seen along the Avon Navigation, as they favour deep and slow-moving water with reedbeds to nest and lay eggs among. Moorhens are the ones with red beaks, coots have white beaks. The chicks of both are scrawny fur balls, moorhen chicks having bright red heads.

Grey heron

"I am but mad north-north-west. When the wind is southerly, I know a hawk from a handsaw".

Hamlet

The Prince of Denmark was protesting his sanity based upon his ability to recognise a *handsaw*, Old English dialect for a grey heron. To be honest, identifying a heron is a pretty

Coot.

low bar. They are unmistakeable, standing motionless over eddy-lines and weir pools hunting for fish, 90 centimetres tall with white underside and blue-grey back. Often you hear their call, *"frank"* before they reveal themselves by taking off with their distinctive slow flapping. Although herons are usually encountered hunting alone, they nest in colonies called heronries, located in treetops. There is a large heronry in Charlecote Park, with about twenty nesting pairs.

Kingfishers

"Expect Saint Martin's summer, halcyon days".

Henry VI Part I

The phrase "halcyon days" references Greek mythology, where a goddess was transformed into a *halcyon* – a kingfisher – with the power to calm the weather. In England, the phrase has come to associate this stunning bird with fine weather and the best of times*. The sudden startling flash of turquoise blue and bright orange, glimpsed as a kingfisher darts downriver, is a commonplace experience whilst paddling the Avon. Much less commonplace, is seeing a kingfisher make its incredibly sleek and precise headfirst dive to catch a fish; the key here is to wait and watch, once a kingfisher has been located. Kingfishers nest in single excavated holes on vertical riverbanks, with an entrance only 6cm across. These can be distinguished from sand martin nests, which have larger entrances and are usually part of a colony.

Mute white swans

"So doth the swan her downy cygnets save, Keeping them prisoner underneath her wings".

Henry VI Part I

Since Shakespeare was dubbed, *"The Sweet Swan of Avon"* by Ben Jonson, these graceful but aggressively territorial birds have become synonymous with the Avon. There were around a hundred at Stratford in the 1950s, and the population of 60 in 1964 was deemed healthy enough to send a dozen to California. Then, their population crashed dramatically, with only three or four remaining by 1979. Fishermen's discarded lead weights were poisoning the birds; swans delve for grit to grind down weeds in their gizzard, and were swallowing the weights. Death was slow and distressing; muscle wastage meant that they eventually couldn't raise their necks to feed themselves. It was also noted that the population on the river below Stratford halved after dredging to restore the Navigation.

The lead weights were banned (although larger 'ledger' weights are still legal, and cause deaths) and the Avon Swan Reserve at Stratford has helped the population to become re-established. Their population on the Upper Avon seems particularly healthy; the author was squeezing his kayak through a gap in reeds near Rugby when a pair suddenly flew in and blocked the way ahead; he was forced to wait directly in front of them, unable to back out, until they had completed a loud and frenetic bout of humping.

*A "Saint Martin's summer" is what we'd now call an Indian Summer.

Reserves and sites

Below are examples of sites along the Avon which have been preserved or restored, representing a range of habitats.

Brandon Marsh SSSI Nature Reserve SP 389 750 – Wetlands in huge area of reclaimed gravel pits along the river right bank, near Ryton-on-Dunsmore. Extensive reedbeds, 237 species of bird recorded! This stretch of the river is overgrown and unpaddleable.

Hampton Wood and Meadow Nature Reserve SP 258 600 – Water meadow and wetland on river right, downstream of Barford. Wetland plants include hemlock, creeping buttercup and meadowsweet.

Lench Meadows LWS (Local Wildlife Site) SP 210 555 – Water meadows, wetlands, wet woodland and other habitats along the river right bank of the Avon, just upstream of Stratford-upon-Avon's centre. Covered with great willowherb, many willows. Otters are known to have been present.

Avon Valley LWS SP 066 477 – Wetlands and wet woodland, scattered across fifteen islands and bank sites along the river (including around Harvington Lock), between Bidford-on-Avon and Tewkesbury. Was the last notable breeding site of the marsh warbler, which has sadly departed. Other species of warbler still present.

Littleton Meadows LWS SP 068 473 – Near Offenham Lock. Water meadows, woodland and pasture, used as hay meadows.

Avon Meadows Community Wetlands and Local Nature Reserve SO 952 461 – At Pershore, developed after the 2007 floods. Water meadows, wetlands, wet woodland. Extensive reedbeds along the riverbanks.

Gwen Finch Wetland Reserve SO 940 420 – Reclaimed wetlands near Nafford Lock on river right. 150,000 reeds and 1,200 willows have been planted! Redshank and lapwing nest here, otters present. Reed bunting, sedge and reed warblers all present. No public access. The John Bennett Wetland Reserve is adjacent and was created since 2009 on clay works from the Pershore Flood Alleviation Scheme.

Upham Meadow and Summer Leasow SSSI SO 917 375 – Also known as Twyning Meadow. Common land, across the river from Bredon. Huge water meadows with the biggest population of curlews in the South West.

Severn Ham SSSI SO 885 325 – The island separating Tewkesbury and the Mill Avon from the River Severn. Common land, one of the last few traditionally-managed water meadows. The Ham is grazed in winter and the hay auctioned by July 12th, then the grass is left for another month before 'Aftermath' when it is auctioned again. Reed buntings present. The only breeding site of corn buntings in the region.

Further Reading

"To pore upon a book, to seek the light of truth."

Love's Labour's Lost

Useful books

A Postcard from Shakespeare's Avon, Jan Dobrzynski and Keith Turner, The History Press Ltd, 2009, ISBN 9780750948487

Exploring Warwickshire's Wild Places, Linda Barnett and Craig Emms, S.B. Publications, 1998, ISBN 1857701607

In Search of Shakespeare, Michael Wood, BBC Books, 2003, ISBN 9780563521419

Moods of Warwickshire and Shakespeare Country, Van Greaves, Halsgrove, 2007, ISBN 9781841145300

Severn and Avon, Lawrence Garner, Landmark, 2008, ISBN 9781843063902

Shakespeare, Bill Bryson, HarperCollins, 2007, ISBN 9780007197903

Shakespeare: a Life, Park Honan, Oxford University Press, 2000, ISBN 9780192825278

Shakespeare Country: Warwickshire, Robin Jones, Halsgrove, 2010, ISBN 9781841149325

Shakespeare's Avon, the History of a Navigation, Jamie Davies, The Oakwood Press, 1996, ISBN 0853614903

Shakespeare's Avon, a journey from Source to Severn, Rob Talbot and Robin Whiteman, Penguin, 1989, ISBN 9780670824960

Shakespeare's Avon Way, a Walk through History, Jenny Davidson, The Macmillan Way Association, 2008, ISBN 0952685167

Sweet Swan of Avon: Rivers in Shakespeare in *SEL Studies in English Literature 1500-1900*, David Bevington and Stephen Bevington, Johns Hopkins University Press, 2019, ISSN 0039-3657

The Gloucestershire Floods 2007, Gill Thomas and Sue Wilson, Sutton Publishing, 2007, ISBN 9780750949460

The Great Gloucestershire Flood 2007, Matt Holmes, Gloucestershire Media, 2007, ISBN 9780752445861

The Nature of Warwickshire, Andy Tasker, Barracuda, 1990, ISBN 0860234738

The Nature of Worcestershire, G.H. Green and Brett Westwood, Barracuda, 1991, ISBN 0860234878

The River Avon, a journey following the river from Tewkesbury to its source, John Bradford, Hunt End Books, 2006, ISBN 9780954981310

The River Avon – a Pictorial History, Josephine Jeremiah, Phillimore & Co. Ltd, 1999, ISBN 9781860771163

The River Avon – Navigation and Visitor Guide, Dutch Lewis, Avon Navigation Trust, 2014

Historical sources

A journey down the Avon is arguably enhanced by knowing what earlier folk experienced, and how they viewed the river. The following accounts are among those cited in this guidebook:

Camping by Water, Noel Carrington and Patricia Cavendish, 1950

Canoeing, William Bliss, 1934

Canoeing, W.G. Luscombe and L.J. Bird, 1948

Canoe Tours in The 1940's and 50s, ed. June Pearton, 2021

Guide to the Waterways of the British Isles, British Canoe Union, 1936

Picturesque Views on the Upper, or Warwickshire Avon, Samuel Ireland, 1795

Portraits of Rivers, ed. Eileen Molony, 1953

Rambles by Rivers: The Avon, James Thorne, 1845

Shakespeare's Avon, from source to Severn, Charles Showell, 1901

The Book of Canoeing, Alec R. Ellis, 1935

The Diary of a Rowing Tour from Oxford to London, Howard Williams, 1875

The Heart of England by Waterway, William Bliss, 1933

The Idyllic Avon, John Henry Garrett, 1906

The Rivers and Streams of England, Arthur Granville Bradley, 1909

The Warwickshire Avon, Sir Arthur Quiller-Couch, 1892

Waterways to Avon, Charles Hadfield and John Norris, 1962

Essential reading

It would be extremely unwise – dangerous, even – to venture by paddlecraft onto the Avon without being fully conversant with this 1,424-page manual, which should also be carried on the water at all times:

The Complete Works of William Shakespeare, William Shakespeare, Oxford, 2005, ISBN 978-0199267187

Offenham.

Index

A

Abbey Bell Tower 117, 124
Abbey Bridge 105, 115, 117, 156
Abbey Mill 13, 147
Abbey Mill Weir 147
Abbey Park 15
access 41, 42
Aickman, Robert 103, 109
All Saints Church, Luddington 97
All Saints Church, Sherborne 77
Alveston 71, 80, 155
Alveston Weir 13, 20, 80
anglers 30
angling season 23
Arch, Joseph 76
Arrow, River 13, 108
Ashow 15, 60, 154
Avon Lock 34, 41, 145, 148
Avon Meadows Community Wetland 116, 156, 183
Avon Navigation 20, 23, 25, 27, 28, 30, 35, 36, 41, 168
Avon Navigation Trust 29, 31, 32, 33, 41, 43, 88, 170, 176
Avon Ring, the 91
Avon, River 17
Avon Swan Reserve 86, 182
Avon, Upper 18, 23, 25, 27, 29, 35, 42
Avon Valley Local Wildlife Site 183

B

Bailey Bridge 145
Bambury Stones 135
Bancroft Basin 87, 88, 91
Bancroft Gardens 15, 88
Bardolatry 93, 171
Barford 71, 73, 76, 155
Barford Bridge 76
Barford Weir 13, 76
barrels 25
Barton Lock 34, 35, 101
Barwell, Douglas 170
Battle of Edgehill 168
Battle of Evesham 108, 111, 117, 124, 166
Battle of Naseby 50, 168
Battle of Tewkesbury 20, 148, 149, 166
Beaufort Bridge 148
Bidford Bridge 95, 102, 105, 106, 155
Bidford Grange islands 13
Bidford Grange Lock 34, 101
Bidford-on-Avon 95, 102, 113
Binton Bridges 13, 95, 99, 103, 155
birds 181
Birlingham 134
Birlingham Wharf 134
Birthplace, The 92, 93
Bloody Meadow 148, 149
boats, powered 30
boats, rowing 30
Borough Flour Mills 146
Brandon Castle 56
Brandon Marsh Nature Reserve 57, 178, 180, 183
Bredon 138, 143, 156
Bredon Great Barn 15, 143
Bredon Ham 142
Bredon Hill 13, 35, 110, 132, 135, 164
Bretford Bridge 53, 56, 154
Brett Young, Francis 120
bridges, hazards 29
British Canoeing 41, 43

Bubbenhall 53, 57, 59, 61, 154
Bubbenhall Bridge 61
buoyancy 26
buoyancy aids 26

C

Caesar's Tower 69, 74
cagoules 26
camping 159
campsites 35
campsites, list of 160
Canal & River Trust 41, 43, 88
canoes 24
Castle Bridge 68, 73
Castle Park 13
Chadbury Lock 13, 34, 118
Chadbury Weir 13, 119
Charlecote Mill 78
Charlecote Park 15, 78, 79, 167
Charles I 50
Chesford Bridge 60, 65, 155
Church of St Pete, Welford-on-Avon 103
Citrus Hotel 154
Cleeve Hill 164
Cleeve Lock 108
Cleeve Mill 13
Cleeve Mill Weir 13
Cleeve Prior 15, 105, 108, 155
climate 20
Clopton Bridge 81, 86, 87
clothing 26
Cloud Bridge 62
Colin P. Witter Lock 90
Comberton Quay 131
Comyns, Barbara 107
coots 181
Corelli, Marie 91

craft, powered 30
Cress Hill 13
Cromwell Memorial 15, 50
Cromwell, Oliver 50
Cromwell, Thomas 167
Cropthorne 15, 122
Cropthorne Mill 13, 121
Crown Meadow 155

D

damselflies 180
Defford Quay Marina 140
Defford Railway Bridge 140
Defford Road Wharf 130
Dissolution of the
    Monasteries
    167
distances 35
Doggy Paddle 81
dragonflies 180
drybags 25
Duke of Edinburgh's Awards
    36

E

Eckington 15, 142
Eckington Bridge 13, 127,
    128, 134, 137, 139, 156, 173
Eckington Sluice 141
Eckington Wharf 134
Elsie and Hiram Billington
    Lock 101
English Civil War 50, 167
entrapment 26
environmental issues 175
equipment 26
equipment, carrying 25
Evesham 105, 106, 112, 115,
    117, 155, 156, 169
Evesham Abbey 113, 117,
    124, 165, 167
Evesham Lock 34, 35, 41, 112
Evesham River Festival 112
Evesham Weir 112
expeditions 35

F

Fladbury 115, 116, 121, 156
Fladbury Lock 13, 34, 121
Fladbury Mill 121
Fladbury Mill Meadow 156
Fladbury Paddle Club 120
Fladbury Weir 121, 122
floods 21, 32
flotation 26
flowers 178
flows 20, 32
footwear 26

G

Garrick, David 92
gauge, river level 32
Gaveston's Cross 65
gear, carrying 25
geology 163
George Billington Lock 110
Gloucester 35
Gordon Gray Lock 96
Gower Monument 88
Grand Union Canal 48, 68
Great Bridge, Pershore 129
Great Comberton 15, 131, 132
grey heron 181
Guy of Warwick 67
Guy's Cave 67
Guy's Cliffe 163
Guy's Cliffe House 15, 67
Gwen Finch Wetland Reserve
    133, 180, 183
GWR Bridge 97

H

habitats 177
Hampton Ferry 117, 156
Hampton Lucy 71, 78, 155
Hampton Lucy Weir 78
Hampton Wood and Meadow
    Nature Reserve 183
Harvington Lock 13, 34, 108
Harvington Weir 13, 108
Hathaway, Anne 92

hazards 26, 29
Healing's Mill 146
helmets 26
help, seeking 31
Henry III 124
Henry VIII 167
heron, grey 181
Hill Wootton Road 155
history 164
Holy Trinity Church,
    Stratford-upon-Avon 89

I

Industrial Age, the 168
Inland Waterways
    Association 109
Inland Waterways
    Association Lock 107
insurance 41
invasive species, non-native
    177

J

Jubilee Bridge 116, 122, 156

K

kayaks 24
kayaks, inflatable 25
Kenilworth 65
kingfishers 182
King John's Bridge 145
King's Newnham Tower 56

L

launch points 153
Leam, River 68
Leicester Tower 15, 118
Lench Meadows Local
    Wildlife Site 183
levels, water 23, 25, 31
licenses 41
Lilbourne 47, 50, 154
Little Lawford 56
Little Meadow River Park 156
Littleton Meadows Local
    Wildlife Site 183

locks 33
locks, keys 34
locks, operating 33
Lower Avon Navigation Trust 170
Lower Lode 35, 137, 139, 145, 148, 150, 156
Lower Lode Inn 156
Lower Lode Lock 41
Lucy's Mill Bridge 90, 91
Lucy's Mill Weir(s) 13, 28, 90, 96
Luddington 97
Luddington Lock 34, 98
Luddington Weir 98

M

Mackay, Mary 91
Maisemore 35, 150
maps 39
Marlcliff 105, 155, 164
Marlcliff Corner 13, 107
Marlcliff Lock 34, 107
Marlcliff Weir 107
meadows, water 178
Middle Ages, the 165
Middle Littleton 15, 110
Middle Littleton tithe barn 110
Mill Avon, the 13, 145, 146
Montfort, Simon de 113, 118, 124, 166
moorhens 181
multi-day trips 35
mute white swans 182

N

Nafford Island 134
Nafford Lock 34, 132
Nafford Weir 13, 132, 133
Naseby 18, 39, 47, 154
Naseby Reservoir 48
National Trust 78, 79, 110, 144, 170
nature reserves 183
Navigation, Avon 20, 23, 25, 27, 28, 30, 35, 36, 41, 168

Newbold on Avon 47, 53, 54, 154
New Bridge, Pershore 130, 156
New Lock 109
non-native invasive species 177

O

obstacles 29
Offenham 15, 106, 111, 155
Offenham Lock 34, 109, 110
Offenham Weir 105, 110, 155
Old Bathing Place, the 72, 81, 155
Ordnance Survey maps 39
Osier Island 13, 123
otters 180
Owen, Richard 164

P

paddleboarding 36
paddleboards 24
paddlecraft 24
Parson's Folly 135
Percy Pilcher RN, Lieutenant 49
Perrott, family 125
Perrott, George 169
Perrott House 125
Pershore 115, 116, 124, 125, 127, 128, 156
Pershore Abbey 15, 125, 129, 165, 167
Pershore Lock 34, 124, 128
Pershore Weir 129
phones, mobile 26
Pilgrim Lock 101
plants 178
playspots 28, 91
pollution 176
portage trails 33
portaging 29, 33
prehistory 164
Public Right of Navigation (PRN) 41

Q

Quay Street Bridge 146
Quiller-Couch, Arthur (Q) 173

R

Recreation Ground, Pershore 115, 116, 124, 127, 156
Recreation Ground, Stratford-upon-Avon 71, 73, 85, 86, 95, 155
Rennie, John 64
reserves, wildlife 183
responsibilities 43
River Arrow 13, 108
River Avon 17
riverbanks (habitat) 178
River Leam 68
river level gauge 32
River Severn 20, 35, 145, 148, 150
River Sowe 68
River Stour 97
River Swilgate 148
river users 30
Robert Aickman Lock 109
Romans, the 165
Royal Leamington Spa 68
Royal Leamington Spa Canoe Club 81
Royal Pump Room Gardens 69
Royal Shakespeare Theatre 15, 81, 85, 86, 89, 96
Rugby 18, 50, 53, 54
rules of the river 32
Ryton Bridge 53, 57
Ryton-on-Dunsmore 57

S

safety 25
Sandy, William 170
Sausage Island 96
Saxon Mill 13, 66
Severn Ham 13, 146, 178, 183

189

Severn, River 20, 35, 145, 148, 150
Shakespeare Birthplace Trust 93
Shakespeare Jubilee 92
Shakespeare Marina 96
Shakespeare's Avon Way 39
Shakespeare, William 17, 19, 92, 113, 167
sites, wildlife 183
sit-on-tops (SOTs) 24
sluices, hazard 28
Smith's Meadow 116, 156
Source, the 47
South Littleton 110
Sowe, River 68
St Andrew's Church, Cleeve Prior 108
stand-up paddleboards (SUPs) 24
Stanford Hall 47, 49, 154, 167
Stanford Park 49
Stanford Reservoir 47, 49, 154
Stare Bridge 59, 62, 154
St Giles' Church, Bredon 143
St Nicholas Park 59, 61, 68, 71, 155
Stoneleigh 68
Stoneleigh Abbey 15, 63, 66, 167
Stoneleigh Deer Park 13, 62, 63
Stour, River 97
Stratford Big Wheel 87
Stratford Canal Basin 88
Stratford River Festival 86
Stratford Trinity Lock 28, 34, 90, 96
Stratford-upon-Avon 20, 35, 71, 73, 81, 85, 92, 95
Stratford-upon-Avon Canal 41, 91, 169, 170
Stratford Waterways Information Centre 41, 88
Strensham Lock 13, 34, 35, 137, 140, 156
Strensham Weir 141
sun protection 26
swans, mute white 182
Swan's Neck 134
Swilgate, River 148

T

Tewkesbury 20, 39, 41, 137, 139, 146, 151, 156, 169
Tewkesbury Abbey 15, 147, 151, 165, 167
Tewkesbury Marina 145
Tiddesley Wood 131
Tiddington 72, 81, 155
Tiddle Widdle Island 13, 123
tithe barn, Bredon 15, 143
tithe barn, Middle Littleton 110
tithe barns 165
trails, portage 33
Tramway Bridge 81, 87, 88
trolley, portage 33
Twyning Green 139, 144, 156

U

Upham Meadow 178, 183
Upper Avon 18, 23, 25, 27, 29, 35, 42
Upper Avon Navigation Trust 170
Upper Lode Lock 148, 149, 150
Upper Lode Weir 149

V

Vale of Evesham 108
voles, water 180

W, X, Y, Z

W. A. Cadbury Lock 100
Wars of the Roses 149, 166
Warwick 74
Warwick Castle 15, 69, 73, 74, 166
Wasperton 77
water levels 23, 25, 31
water meadows 178
Waterside Gardens 155
water voles 180
Webb Ellis, William 50
Weir Brake Lock 34, 96
weirs, hazard 26, 27, 28
Welford 47, 48, 154
Welford Lock 13, 34, 99, 100
Welford-on-Avon 15, 99, 103
Welford Weir 13, 100
Weston-on-Avon 99
wetlands 178
wetsuits 26
wet woodlands 179
white water 19, 28, 29, 59, 85, 91, 133
wildlife 175
willows 181
wind 30
Wolston 53, 56, 154
woodlands, wet 179
Wood Norton Hall 120
Workman Bridge 112
Wyre Lock 34, 35, 123
Wyre Mill 124
Wyre Piddle 116, 123, 156
Wyre Piddle Lock 35

Canoe & Kayak Sales & Hire
Canoe & Kayak Equipment
Outdoor Equipment
Outdoor Clothing

summittosea.co.uk

Unit 10a Penrhos Industrial Estate, Holyhead,
Ynys Mon / Anglesey, LL65 2UQ
e: info@summittosea.co.uk t: +44(0)1407 740963

Venture by pyranha

SINCE 1971

#JustAddVenture

Each and every Venture Canoe & Kayak is designed and built in the UK by the same team behind Pyranha Whitewater Kayaks and P&H Sea Kayaks; our experience dates back to 1971, and our passion for canoeing and kayaking further still, with both flowing through everything we do today.

Part of the Pyranha Family

Made by Enthusiasts for Enthusiasts

Simply Designed for Adventure

Built to a Standard, Not a Price

Advanced Polymer Construction

venturekayaks.com
Designed in the UK & US, built in Great Britain